350AC
110

The NEW ESSENCE *of*
CHRISTIANITY

OTHER BOOKS BY WILLIAM HAMILTON

The NEW ESSENCE *of* CHRISTIANITY

by

William Hamilton

ASSOCIATION PRESS   New York

To My Wife

Preface

In a faculty colloquium at Cornell University in 1964 I found the chair taken for me by a Professor William Hamilton from nearby Colgate Rochester Divinity School. I sensed at once an instinctive sympathy of understanding and an acuteness and astringency of criticism such as make for a really creative relationship. I then remembered that I had in my bag a book of his, *The New Essence of Christianity,* which I had been told a few days earlier that I must get. I read it on my return to England and found it chimed in so accuratedly with the mood of my own lectures on *The New Reformation?* that it was difficult to refrain from pointing them up with frequent quotations from it.

I use the word "mood" advisedly. For I think the significance of Professor Hamilton's book is that it catches, as no other book I know, the "style" in which Christian thinking and living will increasingly have to be done today. Drawing on a wide acquaintance with contemporary literature, he senses the reserve, the humility, the brokenness, which, if we are honest, must characterize

5

our speech in theology, as in science and the arts. He is not building a system for all time. He is reconstructing a house of faith in which a man of this generation can actually live. And it is a house, he freely admits, which has "six storm windows to cover eight windows."

Since this book was first written, Professor Hamilton has himself been pitched into the storm-center of the debate in American Christianity on the "death of God theology." As rumbles from this increase, frequently in its most negative and threatening aspects, it is good that readers still have the chance to appreciate the profoundly positive and sensitive concern that lies behind it.

I do not find myself ending up in the same place as Bill Hamilton. Indeed, he was gracious enough to say in a recent letter: "The thing I am grateful for in your writing is your ability to distinguish between where you are and where others are, and your willingness to let others have their freedom even if they differ wildly from you." I am with him in rating this freedom much higher than agreement. Integrity is a more fundamental virtue in a theologian than orthodoxy. And I count it a privilege to have been asked to write this preface, because I recognize in Bill Hamilton a theologian of integrity, prepared to follow the argument wherever it leads, to whom it would be a disaster if churchmen ceased to listen because they were able to persuade themselves that he was "on the way out."

JOHN WOOLWICH

Contents

Chapter One

CHAPTER 1

On Theological Style

I mean that theology which searches out the nut from the shell, the grain from the husk, the marrow from the bone.—Luther

The sky above us is dark, and this small circle of light barely enables us to see where to place our feet for the next step.—Silone

The phrase "essence of Christianity" evokes certain stereotyped associations that should be noted and then set aside in order to get at the meaning of the phrase as this book proposes to use it. I refer to such ideas as liberating the simple Gospel from superfluous theological accretions, separating the kernel from the husk, finding the eternally valid in the midst of the historical and transient. When these ideas are operative, "essence of Christianity" has often implied that the meaning of the Christian faith can be stated in a form, once and for all, that time and place can never change.

It may be that modern theology needed to react against this way of looking for the "essence of Christianity," but it is not at all clear that the phrase itself does not still have some real usefulness. It is interesting that in Dietrich Bonhoeffer's final papers we have a projected outline for a little book that was to have been called *The Essence of Christianity*. And in the notes for that book, there are few of the traditional themes that we associate with such a title, but rather an interpretation of man's religious situation and a project for a fresh understanding of the humanity of Jesus.[1]

In a formal sense, of course, there is only one essence of Christianity. It is Jesus Christ.[2] But this does not get us very far. We need to say a bit more about what "essence of Christianity" might mean for us, and why it may prove to be a useful form for the presentation of theology in our day. Is there not a time and a place for the right kind of theological reduction? Isn't it sometimes useful to try to state those few affirmations that seem unmistakably clear, without which we cannot live or think as Christians? Such a modest venture would not deliver *the* essence, once and for all, but rather *an* essence here and now for us—always ready to be corrected

---

[1] This outline is found on pp. 178-81 of *Letters and Papers from Prison* (London: SCM Press, 1953), published in the U. S. under the title *Prisoner of God* (New York: Macmillan Co.). See also Eberhard Bethge, "The Editing and Publishing of the Bonhoeffer Papers," *The Andover Newton Bulletin*, LII, No. 2 (December, 1959), p. 3. My essay as a whole is deeply indebted to Bonhoeffer, and may be taken as a theological response to the coming of age of the world as he has analyzed it.

[2] This is the conclusion to the essay "The Permanent Element in Christianity," by Anders Nygren, translated recently by Philip S. Watson and included in a little book called, interestingly, *Essence of Christianity* (London: Epworth Press, 1960), pp. 49, 55.

by other interpretations and other visions that see, believe, and love more widely than any one man is able to do.

What would such an essence involve? Before we come to the theological content itself, there are several proto-theological factors of some importance. "Essence of Christianity" today, stripped of its dangers, implies, for one thing, a certain kind of theological style, and this style may be divided into a question about structure and form and a question about the tone of our theological speech. In this chapter we will take up these questions in turn.

FRAGMENT AS OUR THEOLOGICAL FORM

I suspect that we have come to a time when theology should try to give up its structural pretensions and be content with not much more than a collection of fragments or images, not too precisely related to each other, indirectly rather than directly put forth.[3] This structural suggestion has not commended itself to many in our time, for ours is a day of confidence, of the intellectual offensive; large books; dogmatic and philosophical theology; word-study and exegesis. In face of this current mood, a

---

[3] Something of this sense of what theology is can be found in an article by Jacob Taubes, who stated that "the time has come perhaps when theology must learn to live without the support of canon and classical authorities. Without authority, however, theology can only teach by an indirect method.... Theology would have to remain incognito and not strive for the vainglory to present itself as exegesis of canonic scriptures and classical creeds." "Theology and the Philosophic Critique of Religion," *Cross Currents*, V, No. 4 (Fall, 1955).

theology of fragments must seem unnecessary, timid, and even dangerous. But perhaps we need both Cadillacs and Volkswagens on our theological highways; each has things it can and cannot do. For those who cannot manage well-ordered and confident theological prose, a little disorder and some fragmentariness may be useful.

The form and structure of a new essence of Christianity will be fragmentary. But are we willing to pay the price for this? This will mean living with very little theological security, in half-finished houses, with many things left unsaid because they are, for the moment, unsayable. This will mean running a real risk of robbing the Gospel of some of its power, or dishonestly putting forth a reduced Gospel so that modern man may be able to grasp it without so much difficulty. But to give up our longing for the whole truth, and to fasten on the little truth that we can get clear may enable us, for all the risks, to catch accurately a particular mood in our culture that can be interpreted theologically in no other way.[4] But a theology that refuses to have something to say about everything will rightly be very vulnerable to critical attack. And it will never be valid for an extended period of time. The fragmentary essence in this essay begins, properly (in Chapter 2), with a description of believing man as he stands before God today. It has as

---

[4] "I must confess that after all these years I am still concerned with the veritable rather than with the whole Gospel. This is because only by laying hold of the veritable Gospel does it seem to me to be possible to reach out towards the whole Gospel." Karl Barth, *The Epistle to the Romans* (London: Oxford University Press, 1933), p. 12 (from the Preface to the second edition, written in 1921).

its center a Christological affirmation (Chapter 3); and
it concludes with some ethical consequences (Chapter
4). I am setting down this essence, this vision, to get it
clear for myself; to elicit other visions that can correct
and fill the gaps in this one; and in general to explore the
possibility of doing our theological work today with as
little baggage as possible.

One strand in modern Protestant thought has some
affinity with the line I am taking. I refer to the idea of
"the essence of Christianity" that is associated with the
late nineteenth and early twentieth centuries. We can
best understand this tradition by looking first at that
curious and fascinating scholar, Ludwig Feuerbach, who
published, in 1841, a book entitled *The Essence of Christianity*.[5] Many know Feuerbach today only because of
his influence on Karl Marx, but he was in his own way
an original, if eccentric, theologian. His "essence" is simply stated. Feuerbach was in violent disagreement with
the idealism of his day (largely the school of Hegel)
which ignored the concrete man of flesh and blood in
favor of man as abstract mind or ego, and which located
God among the abstract conceptions of the mind rather
than in the world of man. His task, as he saw it, was to
transform theology into anthropology. What Christianity ascribed to God must be ascribed to man; the perfections of God must become the perfections of man and his

---

[5] In German, *Das Wesen des Christentums*. A useful reprinting of
this work, with an important introductory essay by Karl Barth, has
recently been issued: Ludwig Feuerbach, *The Essence of Christianity*
(New York: Harper & Bros., 1957).

society. The nature of God he did not deny or ignore; it was simply identical with the nature of man. Man's divinity was the aim of Christian thought and life.

Feuerbach loved to quote the saying that one finds in many of the early church fathers, that God became man so that man might become God. And while we retreat in embarrassment from this phrase, he tried to take it seriously. He quoted often from Luther, and always to telling effect, in making his simple point: "The deeper we can bring Christ into the flesh, the better." "God himself, when he is dealt with out of Christ, is a terrible God for no consolation is found in him, but pure anger and disfavor." [6]

Feuerbach's "essence" was thus both philosophical and practical. Philosophically, it was determined by a radical anti-idealism, an attempt (made in other ways by Marx and Kierkegaard) to stand Hegel on his head. Practically, it was determined by a passion for the welfare of man in a culture where theology and philosophy alike ignored his flesh-and-blood reality.

About sixty years after Feuerbach's "essence" was published, another book appeared in German with the identical title, *Das Wesen des Christentums*, by the dis-

---

[6] These quotations are on p. 49 of *The Essence of Christianity*. Both the theological and the literary worlds are restudying Feuerbach today. An interesting study of him is found in Henri de Lubac, *The Drama of Atheist Humanism* (London: Sheed & Ward, 1949); and in *Nineteenth Century Studies* (New York: Columbia University Press, 1949), Basil Willey has pointed to the profound effect Feuerbach had on the religious rebels of the Victorian period. George Eliot was the translator of *The Essence of Christianity*, and this book decisively shaped her own religious position.

tinguished German historian and biblical scholar Adolf Harnack.[7] His purpose was to reject the possibility of any philosophical reduction of Christianity to its essentials. There was only one way to get to the heart of the matter, and that was by a purely historical description of primitive Christianity and of how it had been transformed in the intervening centuries.

Historical investigation alone will enable us to see for ourselves the essence, to separate the kernel from the husk, and it tells us two things, Harnack claimed. First, it gives us a reasonably clear picture of Jesus' impact on his own times; second, it shows us that this impact was blurred, altered, and even distorted by the centuries that followed the first. When we penetrate back, beyond the weeds that have grown up around the original flower, we have a very simple and powerful truth. This truth Harnack put in several ways: "Eternal life in the midst of time, by the strength and under the eyes of God." Or: "In the combination of these ideas—God the Father, Providence, the position of men as God's children, the infinite value of the human soul—the whole Gospel is expressed." [8]

Harnack's influence was very great in the early years of this century, and there were many attempts, using

---

[7] This has also been recently reprinted: Adolf Harnack, *What is Christianity?* (New York: Harper & Bros., 1957). As Karl Barth, feeling the underrated power of Feuerbach, contributed an introductory essay to the reprinting of that book, so Rudolf Bultmann invites us to reconsider Harnack in his introduction to the recent reprinting.

[8] *Op. cit.*, pp. 8, 68.

both his methods and other ones, to find some way of setting forth the essence of Christianity.[9] But since that
time, Harnack has been powerfully attacked on several
fronts. Many today have shed his confidence that the
original meaning of Jesus' message can be recovered at
all by historical means. Others would grant that while
the true content of Jesus' message can in part be histori-
cally described, Harnack in any case completely misread
it. Schweitzer, for example, in *The Quest of the Historical
Jesus,* believed that historical investigation is adequate to
the task of recovering Jesus' message, but the result is
nothing like Harnack's gentle preacher of God's Father-
hood and man's infinite value. It is rather a picture of a
fanatic who believed that his appearance and death would
usher in the Kingdom of God in a catastrophic way. The
very eschatological elements that Harnack had banished
on historical grounds Schweitzer called, on the same
grounds, utterly central to the New Testament. Harnack
found his essence and concluded that it could speak rele-
vantly to any age. Schweitzer saw a completely different
essence and found it quite irrelevant to any age.

Thus, in the first part of this century, there were a
number of different essences, a number of methods proposed for their distillation, and the cultural ideals of the

---

[9] Rudolf Eucken's book *The Truth of Religion* (published origi-
nally in 1905) is a good example. Eucken's essential Christianity was
not unlike Harnack's: a spiritual idea of God and an absolutist conception of value. But his method of arriving at this was more philosophical than historical. For Eucken, the historical was the transitory
part of Christianity: the essence was a particular idea of spirituality
defined in terms of post-Hegelian idealism.

period always affected the essence that was discovered. So it is not surprising that the essence-of-Christianity tradition grinds to a painful halt, and we find Ernst Troeltsch delivering its funeral oration and calling an end to the whole procedure. Neither philosophy nor historical method, he claimed, can give us any theological residuum that we can adopt from the past, without change.[10]

Is there a way out of this theological relativism? Anders Nygren today claims that there is. He attacks historical method as used in the essence-of-Christianity tradition as arbitrary, and proposes that we free ourselves from subjectivity by declaring that Jesus Christ, the atonement, and forgiveness of sins are the true permanent element in Christianity.[11] But does this really face the issue? Can the finite Christian's partial vision be transcended by a theological affirmation? Isn't it a little suspicious that the objective essence Nygren produces sounds very Lutheran? No, we must accept our subjectivity and partial vision, and save ourselves from the errors of the earlier essence-of-Christianity tradition simply by not claiming permanent validity for what we see. All our theology, even our essences of Christianity, must be done afresh in every generation.

---

10 Cf. Troeltsch's article "Was heisst 'Wesen des Christentums?'" first published in *Christliche Welt*, 1903, and later in *Gesammelte Schriften*, II (Tübingen: J.C.B. Mohr Verlag, 1913), pp. 386-451. Also his *Protestantism and Progress*, first published in German in 1906. The 1912 English translation has recently been reprinted by Beacon Press (1958).

11 Nygren, *op. cit.*, pp. 20-1, 49, 55.

This essay, then, tries to be both modest and decisive.
It is largely a series of fragments that may serve, if at all,
only for a limited time and place. It is not sufficient or
adequate, and it needs the fragments and the visions of
others.

THE TONE OF OUR SPEECH

Essence of Christianity entails an invitation to a certain kind of structure and form. But there is another part
of theological style just as important, and that is the matter of the tone of theological language, the way in which
what is seen and believed is communicated or spoken. If
theology as fragmentary essence differs from the theological masters of our day in structure, it differs also on
this subtle matter of tone or rhetoric. For today our
betters not only build and order their work more confidently than we can manage; they also speak more boldly
and assuredly than we can.

The problem of how we speak to one another has been
a concern on the non-theological literary scene for some
time, and we might well touch on some of the things
there being said.[12] One thinks, for example, of T. S.

---

[12] Literary critics have distinguished between the first and second
generation of modern novelists. The giants of the modern novel are,
let us say, Joyce, Proust, and Mann. Their range is wide, their tone
is confident, they have said a great deal about many things, and we
have all learned from them. But the second generation novelists,
Camus and Silone in Europe, Faulkner and Hemingway in this country, differ significantly from the earlier giants. Here there is a retreat
to the knowable, the polishing and perfecting of the little that is
known, the careful attempt not to write and to say everything in
large and confident tones.

Eliot's concern with the breakdown of the words we use
to speak to each other. In "The Hollow Men" he describes the impotence of our speech:

> Our dried voices, when
> We whisper together
> Are quiet and meaningless
> As wind in dry grass
> Or rats' feet over broken glass
> In our dry cellar
> > Shape without form, shade without colour,
> > Paralysed force, gesture without motion;

And in a later work, he moves to a solution.

So here I am. . . .
Trying to learn to use words, and every attempt
Is a wholly new start, and a different kind of failure
Because one has only learnt to get the better of words
For the thing one no longer has to say, or the way in which
One is no longer disposed to say it. And so each venture
Is a new beginning, a raid on the inarticulate
With shabby equipment always deteriorating
In the general mess of imprecision of feeling,
Undisciplined squads of emotion. And what there is to
  conquer
By strength and submission, has already been discovered
Once or twice, or several times, by men who one cannot
  hope
To emulate—but there is no competition—
There is only the fight to recover what has been lost
And found and lost again and again: and now, under
  conditions

That seem unpropitious. But perhaps neither gain nor loss.
For us, there is only the trying. The rest is not our
        business.[13]

In a recent book, Leslie Fiedler has suggested that the
rejection of old words and styles and the struggle for the
new is a normal experience for an American writer.

> Merely finding a language, learning to talk in a land
> where there are no conventions of conversation, no
> special class idioms and no dialogue between classes, no
> continuing literary language—this exhausts the Ameri-
> can writer. He is forever *beginning*, saying for the first
> time (without real tradition there can never be a second
> time) what it is like to stand alone before nature, or in
> a city as appallingly lonely as any virgin forest.[14]

An interesting point here is the relation between style of
speaking and attitude to tradition. Is there something
basically antitraditional about the American, even the
American man of faith? If so, such a man must begin to
speak, as if no one had ever spoken before, about that
tradition, and about how he is bound both to take it and
to leave it. This native relation to tradition may be a
weakness; it may, for instance, make it especially hard to
be a novelist, a Christian, or even a theologian. But it is

---

[13] From "East Coker," in *Four Quartets*, copyright 1943, by T. S.
Eliot. Reprinted by permission of Harcourt, Brace & World, Inc. The
extract from "The Hollow Men" is on p. 56 of the collected works.

[14] Leslie A. Fiedler, *Love and Death in the American Novel* (New
York: Criterion Books, 1960), p. xix.

there, surely, and it cannot be eliminated by a conscious decision to ignore it.

Another contemporary who has faced this problem of how, and under what conditions, one man can speak to another, is the Italian writer Ignazio Silone. Indeed, this may be said to be the theme of all his writing. Without our going over the plot of *Bread and Wine*, the following extracts will give a feeling for Silone's concern:

> "The scourge of our time," calmly replied Dom Bene-detto ... "is insincerity between man and man, lack of faith between man and man...." [15]

To break down this insincerity, Silone says in his novel, men must learn to talk to one another once more. In order to do this, "two men must be alone together, talk softly and with many pauses" (p. 112). Later in the novel, there is another reference to the role of quietness in our speech. "There is a kind of silence," the leading character says, "in which the hard thick shell which normally covers and protects us, the thick shell of fiction and prejudice and ready-made phrases which separate man from man, begins to crack and open. There is no need to fear such silence. There is no need to be afraid of throwing off all formulas, commonplaces, and sententious phrases" (p. 158).

To find once more the right way to speak the truth

---

[15] *Bread and Wine* (New York: Harper & Bros., Penguin Books, 1946), p. 18.

to another man: this is the concern and the hope of such widely different artists as Silone and Eliot.[16] At the close of a recent article, Silone has portrayed his hope in an unforgettable image:

> Our problems are limited in range. We are neither believers nor atheists, nor are we sceptics. . . . What is left in the end? There are, it seems to me, a few Christian certainties so deeply immured in human existence as to be identified with it. Anyhow I do not think I have the right to speak of faith, but only of a certain trust. This trust is founded and turns on something more than the compassion of Albert Camus. It is founded on the inner certainty that we are free and responsible, and it turns on the absolute need of finding a way towards the inmost reality of other people. . . . Humbly we must confess that we have no panacea. All we have —and it is a great deal—is this trust that makes it pos-

---

[16] One can't help but be reminded of the work of Martin Buber at this point. But there is a curious phrase of Bonhoeffer's that can perhaps correct some dangers in Buber's work, or at least in the use Christians have made of him. He speaks of the need to "fight for a revival of a wholesome reserve between man and man" (*Letters and Papers from Prison*, p. 22). The context in which this occurs is not easy to get clear, but perhaps we can take it to mean that there are times in personal relationships when one must not attempt to deal with the other as a Thou. He must at times be allowed his freedom to remain an "it," a silence, a mystery, over against me. The reserve of which Bonhoeffer speaks, then, serves as a kind of timing device for personal encounters, lest they move too swiftly and too heedlessly into depths for which they are unprepared. Silone's idea of a necessary silence as part of our authentic speech comes very close to Bonhoeffer's defense of reserve, though Bonhoeffer does not apply his remark, as I am doing, to our theological speech. Below, on pp. 123-24 I refer again to these words of Bonhoeffer.

sible for us to go on living. The sky above us is dark, and this small circle of light barely enables us to see where to place our feet for the next step.

This amounts to saying that the spiritual situation I have just described admits neither of defence nor of arrogance. Frankly, it is merely an expedient. It resembles a refugee encampment in no-man's-land, an exposed makeshift encampment. What do you think refugees do from morning to night? They spend most of their time telling one another the story of their lives. The stories are anything but amusing, but they tell them to one another, really, in an effort to make themselves understood. As long as there remains a determination to understand and to share one's understanding with others, perhaps we need not altogether despair.[17]

Two things in this passage seem to me relevant to this matter of the tone of our theological speaking. The first is the image of standing in the dark, with only a bit of light enabling us to see the next step. We do not have, I think, enough faith or enough truth to satisfy us, but only enough to get on with. What more will come depends, of course, on God's grace; but this grace is more likely to be known if we get on with what we have. The second image completes and corrects the first. It is the image of the makeshift encampment of refugees. We are,

---

[17] From Silone's "The Choice of Comrades," first published in English in *Encounter* (London), December, 1954, and later collected in the paperback volume *Voices of Dissent* (New York: Grove Press, 1958).

after all, not alone. There are, somewhere, others whose stories we must hear, and who are humble enough to listen to our stories. Theology is not only just enough to get on with; it is a makeshift camp-site with others present. We are alone; yet there are others there, and we need to know them.

It is because this kind of writing today seems to me so universally true that I have spent some time on the way we speak to each other as a proper theological concern. There is an appropriate style, or rhetoric, for our theological language, and an inappropriate one. And our divergence from our betters is largely on this level, rather than on the level of what they say.

Dr. Oppenheimer, at the close of his Columbia University Bicentennial address, "Prospects in the Arts and Sciences," touches on the same need for being open to one another, the same feeling for the precariousness of our lives in our day. What he here says of the artist and the scientist must surely be said of the theologian and the man of faith.

> This is a world in which each of us, knowing his limitations, knowing the evils of superficiality and the terrors of fatigue, will have to cling to what is close to him, to what he knows, to what he can do, to his friends and his tradition and his love, lest he be dissolved in a universal confusion and know nothing and love nothing. It is at the same time a world in which none of us can find hieratic prescription or general sanction for any ignorance, any insensitivity, any indifference.

...If a man tells us that he sees differently than we or that he finds beautiful what we find ugly, we may have to leave the room, from fatigue or trouble; but that is our weakness and our default. If we must live with a perpetual sense that the world and the men in it are greater than we and too much for us, let it be the measure of our virtue that we know this and seek no comfort. Above all let us not proclaim that the limits of our powers correspond to some special wisdom in our choice of life, of learning, or of beauty.

This balance, this perpetual, precarious, impossible balance between the infinitely open and the intimate, this time—our twentieth century—has been long in coming; but it has come. It is, I think, for us and our children, our only way.... Both the man of science and the man of art live always at the edge of mystery, surrounded by it; both always, as the measure of their creation, have had to do with the harmonization of what is new with what is familiar, with the balance between novelty and synthesis, with the struggle to make partial order in total chaos....

This cannot be an easy life. We shall have a rugged time of it to keep our minds open and to keep them deep, to keep our sense of beauty and our ability to make it, and our occasional ability to see it in places remote and strange and unfamiliar; we shall have a rugged time of it, all of us, in keeping these gardens in our villages, in keeping open the manifold, intricate, casual paths, to help these flourishing in a great, open, windy world; but this, as I see it, is the condition of man; and in this condition we can help, because we can love, one another.[18]

There is more of this kind of chaos and mystery in our lives and thought than we, as Christians, have ordinarily dared to admit. If Dr. Oppenheimer has seen our condition accurately, our theological response to it may well be that we can search for only a provisional order, a makeshift position, a place to stay for a moment before moving on into the darkness.

We must be careful in our defenses of humility. Proud men delight in defending this virtue, and it is notoriously easy to defend it arrogantly. Sometimes, for example, we are advised to be humble theologians so the unbelieving world won't be put off by our arrogance. But a humility put on like a winter coat to keep the wintry, unbelieving world at bay is a very poor garment indeed. We are reduced to fragments, partial vision, broken speech, not because of the unbelieving world "out there," but precisely because that unbelieving world has come to rest within ourselves. We really are reduced to very little. We have the hope of only a little provisional order in our spiritual chaos, as our inadequate minds and spirits try to face the terror both of the world and of God.

What does all this talk about speech and silence have to do with Christian theology? The answer must be fairly clear. Those of us who are trying to make the Christian

---

[18] The address can be found in the *Bulletin of the Atomic Scientists*, XI (February, 1955), pp. 42-4. Used by permission of the Board of Trustees of Columbia University, N. Y.

faith intelligible to ourselves and to others have probably spent too much time and too many words saying that we saw and believed what we did not truly see and believe, and we did not like the experience of having deceived ourselves, even if we deceived no one else. But our reaction was no wiser, for we began to spend even more time declaring what we could not accept and believe, and we thus deprived ourselves of what power we had to live with the little that we did believe. We have taken too much pride in our affirmations, and too much pride in the skill of our denials. Our denials are there, all right, but they are both unimportant and marks of our weakness, and ought to be interesting neither to ourselves nor to anyone else.

I suppose I am fighting the style of Christian thought which believes that Christianity must always be on the offensive. We were tired of being pushed around intellectually, maneuvered into impossible corners, ridiculed by sharp and sensitive minds. So we became sharp and we took up the attack, and something queer happened. We won all kinds of intellectual battles, and made Christianity intellectually respectable on campus, in church, and even in the seminary. But, in going on the offensive, we ourselves became offensive in the other sense, and a note of stridency and harshness crept into our private and public voices. (Have you ever heard a biblical theologian preach?) For some, this meant being at ease in the faculty club and bewildered in the pulpit; for others it meant that student movement conferences are fine, but churches are impossible. In any case, we forgot that our major battle is not with anyone "out there," but with the foolishness, sin, and unbelief in ourselves. We began to read and to be moved by men like Camus, who spoke quietly of these matters and tried to clarify the little he knew rather than to claim to know very much. Philosophically, we found ourselves questioning the strident cries of the existentialist philosopher, forever pushing us into an abyss or into a fear of death or into a meaninglessness that we didn't always feel, and discovering that the more mundane tone of the logical analysts made at least a stylistic sense to us that we hadn't noticed in them before.

We need to reduce the area of what is believed and to lay claim upon it. And we need to learn from anyone, anywhere, who has the time and grace to speak about what he really knows. In this terrible world, anyone with passionate honesty moves us, and unbelief when it has this passion is more attractive to us than belief when it lacks it. The religious revival in our land, the theological productions of the Ecumenical Movement—these are no doubt very important to many people; yet there is too much confident and conventional talking here, and we are not really much interested in either. We have to learn to talk in our own way, no doubt brokenly, less assuredly. We cannot reject the Christian past, or rewrite it in prettier words, as did liberalism. Nor can we swallow it in one large swallow, hoping that if we love Augustine enough we will be given good marks for proper devotion to the tradition. Both orthodoxy and liberalism lose the delicate balance between what we do and can believe, what we do not and cannot believe, and what we may hope to believe. We do not glory in our littleness of faith. It saddens and sickens us, and we seek to increase it in company with whoever will listen and speak in the right way.

But who can claim to know the "right way"? Perhaps it is this: being willing to admit that our knowledge and our faith are in bits and pieces; being content with this weakness; clarifying the little we can know; speaking about it as openly as we can; listening to the other as often as we speak. In this way we may come to a tolerable essence of Christianity for our day.

Philip Toynbee has recently defined the intellectual climate of the twentieth century as a struggle between the dragon-killers and the dragons. Their basic attitudes he describes thus:

> On the one hand a revulsion against loose thinking, pretentious writing, all kinds of insubstantial pageants. A determination to accept the limitations of our knowledge and to pay fitting respect to the commonplace and the everyday. On the other hand a sense that human life has become impoverished and unrewarding, and the determination to take risks, of speculation and of language, in order to restore man to his true stature.[19]

This defense of essence of Christianity stands, I suppose, as a contribution to a theology for dragon-killers. Dragon-killers must always be inexperienced and some-

---

[19] *The Observer* (London), December 20, 1959.

what foolish, while it is in the nature of dragons, as everyone knows, to be aging and confident in the power of their flaming nostrils and lethal tails. The dragon-killer as theologian must be careful, however, that the dragon's love of risk and his concern for man's true stature are not somehow lost along the way.

Let us say no more about fragmentariness; let us turn to some of the fragments themselves. Even a modest essence of Christianity has more than a certain structure and tone; it must have content.

Chapter Two

CHAPTER **2**

Belief in a Time of the
Death of God

*The insurmountable barrier to Christianity does seem to
me to be the problem of evil.*—Albert Camus

The love of God is a hard love.
—Paneloux in Camus' *The Plague*

Most observers would agree that—whatever they might
think of it—there has been in our time a recovery of what
can be called the biblical-Augustinian-Reformed way of
speaking about God. There is a certain oddness about
putting it like this, because one of the main emphases of
this way of speaking is that God cannot really be spoken
of at all. It will be useful to set down a few of the main
characteristics of this tradition, for it is a lively and powerful one that has won the allegiance of most of the
thoughtful and sensitive Christians of our day.

35

OUR CORRECT DOCTRINE OF GOD

A certain idea of revelation is implied in this tradition: the biblical notion that we cannot in ourselves know God, but that he has made himself known to us. In ourselves, we are without God; but he acts, he speaks, he enters into our lives. Karl Barth locates the Bible as the place where God speaks, and he writes, at the beginning of his volume on election:

> We took as our starting-point what God Himself said and still says concerning God, and concerning the knowledge and reality of God, by way of the self-testimony which is accessible and comprehensible because it has been given human form in Holy Scripture.[1]

This note runs throughout Barth's massive writing—a confidence that, however broken and untrustworthy may be the other places where we might expect God to speak, scripture is the special meeting-place between God and man.

For John Baillie, the direction of revelation is the same (from God to us, out of his gracious love), but the meeting-place differs. "To believe in God is to believe that He is present in our company as we tell one another why we believe in Him." And a little later:

> I believe in God because He confronts me with a demand that brooks no refusal. He stands at my heart's

---

[1] *Church Dogmatics*, II/2 (Edinburgh: T. & T. Clark, 1957), p. 3. Published in the U. S. by Chas. Scribner's Sons (N. Y.).

> door and knocks. He is there now. I know quite well
> that He is there, and I know that He wants more of me
> than I have yet given Him. . . . He comes to me indeed
> with a demand, but the demand is only that I should
> accept a gift—the gift of salvation.[2]

God himself speaks to us in scripture; he is standing
now at the door of my heart, and I cannot deny it. God
is known to us because he has spoken. We cannot deny
what we have heard. This is the uniform testimony of
those most qualified to speak today.

And it is fundamental to the entire Christian tradition.
Lying behind this contemporary formulation of how
God is known is an impressive historical pedigree. This
pedigree can be glimpsed if we call attention to Augustine in the Milanese garden (*Confessions*, Book VIII), to
Luther's discovery of a righteous God at Wittenberg,
and to Pascal's "Memorial," the document found sewed
into the lining of his coat after his death. Augustine, for
some months before his "conversion," had called upon
God to heal his divided will, but the healing did not
come. He knew the inadequacy of the alternatives; he
knew what belief in God meant; he even "believed"; but
all of his willing was marred by a not-willing. In a highly
emotional moment, set off by some trivial children's
words in the next yard to his, he opened his New Testament at random, read some words about putting off the
lusts of the flesh, and the impossible happened. He had

---

2 "Why I Believe in God," *Union Seminary Quarterly Review*,
March, 1949.

not been free to will, and he became free because God made him free. Luther, in a moment he describes as the opening of the heavens, moved from a hatred of the demanding God to a joyous acceptance of a forgiving God. Certainty, God speaking, joy. These were the undeniable notes of the "conversion" experiences of both these men.

The themes of Augustine's and Luther's experiences are partly reflected in the famous memorial fragment of Pascal, which records an event that took place on November 23, 1654, some eight years before his death. The record of this decisive experience reads like this.

FIRE

God of Abraham, God of Isaac, God of Jacob, not of the philosophers and scientists
Certainty. Certainty. Feeling. Joy. Peace.
     God of Jesus Christ
     Deum meum et Deum vestrum.
     Thy God shall be my God.
Forgetfulness of the world and of all, except God.
He is to be found only by the ways taught in the Gospel.
     Greatness of the human Soul.
O righteous Father, the world hath not known Thee, but I have known Thee.
          Joy, Joy, Joy, tears of joy.
               I separated myself from Him.
          Dereliquerunt me fontem aquae vitae
          My God, wilt Thou forsake me?
May I never be separated from Him eternally.

"This is life eternal, that they might know Thee the only
true God, and Jesus Christ whom Thou has sent."
> Jesus Christ
> Jesus Christ

I separated myself from Him; I fled Him, renounced Him,
crucified Him.
> May I never be separated from Him!

He is to be kept only by the ways taught in the Gospel:
> Renunciation, entire and sweet.

This passionate statement of Pascal sums up most of
what we have learned to say about the idea of revelation
today. God is a God of Abraham, Isaac, and Jacob—the
biblical God who meets men in critical historical events,
not the philosophical God found at the end of a micro-
scope or the end of an argument. And he meets men who
do not wish to meet him; indeed, he meets men who seek
to flee from him. But when God does break through,
man knows that it has happened, and he finds certainty
and rest and understanding.

This is one theme in the accepted portrait of God
today. There is another, very closely related to the first,
and just as characteristic of what we are calling the Augustinian-Reformed picture of God. This second theme
has to do with the breakdown of the idea of God as a
person or an object, and the attempt to find other forms
of expression. We need, J. H. Oldham writes,

> a new understanding of the fact that we cannot *objec-
> tify* God.... God is not an object among other objects.
> He is not a cause among other causes. He is not, as we
> tend to think of Him, an immensely great and power-

ful person existing alongside of other persons. All these ways of thinking of Him make Him part of the world; He is the creator and sustainer of the world. He does not belong to the objective world at all. When we objectify Him, He ceases to be God. . . . It is true that we cannot, in fact, think or speak of God without objectifying Him. That means that, strictly speaking, we cannot talk about God. We can only talk to Him.[3]

This invitation to put aside our thinking of God as object or person is not so simple as it looks. It is based on the perfectly true observation that when we talk about God, our language gets distorted and broken, and we are bound to sound muddled and even self-contradictory. Augustine knew this well, but concluded that it is better to say contradictory things with as much care as we can, than to remain silent. Others have felt it both safer and wiser to keep silent in speaking about God (the mystic and the atheist reach a curious agreement on this point). Yet if there is to be Christian understanding of God, if there is to be theology at all, we must prefer unwise speaking to prudent silence.

What, then, art Thou, O my God—What, I ask, but the Lord God? For who is Lord but the Lord? or who is God save our God? Most high, most excellent, most potent, most omnipotent; most merciful and most just; most hidden and most near; most beauteous and most strong, stable, yet contained of none; unchangeable, yet changing all things; never new, never old; making

---

[3] *Life is Commitment* (London: SCM Press, 1959), pp. 46-7.

all things new, yet bringing old age upon the proud and they know it not; always working, yet ever at rest; gathering, yet needing nothing; sustaining, pervading and protecting; creating, nourishing, and developing; seeking, and yet possessing all things. Thou lovest, and burnest not; art jealous, yet free from care; repentest, and hast no sorrow; art angry, yet serene; changest Thy ways, leaving unchanged Thy plans; recoverest what Thou findest, having yet never lost; art never in want, whilst Thou rejoicest in gain; never covetous, though requiring usury. That Thou mayest owe, more than enough is given to Thee; yet who hath anything that is not Thine? Thou payest debts while owing nothing; and when Thou forgivest debts, losest nothing. Yet, O my God, my life, my holy joy, what is this that I have said? And what saith any man when he speaks of Thee? Yet woe to them that keep silence, seeing that even they who say most are as the dumb.[4]

We cannot objectify God, but we must speak about him. So we get into trouble, our words become distorted, and we raise questions about his location and behavior that we cannot answer. If we objectify him, we make him part of the world, but a part we cannot see. We make him part of the causal sequences of the world, and try to fit him into the order and disorder that we see. But then we find that we must say that he made the world or that he caused the evil and suffering of the world, or we refuse to say this. And so we have on our hands either a capricious tyrant causing evil as well as

---

[4] Augustine, *Confessions*, I. 4.

good, or an ineffectual thing, impotent before evil and causing only the good. We seek for words that express God as something other than personal, and we fall into the danger of making him less than personal. The God seen as a person, making the world, manipulating some people towards good, condemning other people to damnation—the objectified God, in other words—this is the God many have declared to be dead today. This is the God who must disappear, so that we may remake our thinking and our speaking about him. "The courage to be," Dr. Tillich writes in one of his most elusive and profound statements, "is rooted in the God who appears when God has disappeared in the anxiety of doubt." [5]

These two affirmations suggest the contours of the rediscovered Augustinian-Reformed portrait of God in our time. They point to what might be called a recovery of God's divinity, his holiness, his separateness from men. Each of the two basic statements we used to describe this portrait carried a positive and a negative component. The first declared that we cannot know God, but that he has made himself known to us. The second stated that God cannot be properly spoken of or treated as an object, but that we can still praise, adore, speak to him. Put technically, the generally received portrait of God today supports the Reformed insistence that the finite cannot contain the infinite (*finitum non capax infiniti*) and rejects the Lutheran tradition which declares that in the

---

[5] *The Courage to Be* (New Haven: Yale University Press, 1952), p. 190.

humanity of Jesus the finite has received, and thus can contain, the infinite (*finitum capax infiniti*).[6]

There is a great deal to be said for this rediscovery of the divinity of God, but it may be that we are beginning to pay too dear a price for it. Are we not, perhaps, beginning to lose the delicate balance between negation and affirmation that this position requires? We have come to find it far easier to say "we cannot know" than to say "he can make himself known." His holiness and separateness are beginning to look like an indifference. Now it comes as no great surprise to remind ourselves that the most scrupulously correct theological statements have their own built-in difficulties. One of the reasons why theological moods change is that men come to a time when they want to live with new kinds of difficulties. Theology is always like having six storm windows to cover eight windows. One is quite free to choose which six windows to keep the cold air from entering, and you can live pretty well for a while in the protected rooms. But the uncovered windows will let the cold air in sooner

---

[6] Eberhard Bethge has recently noted that the Lutheran *finitum capax infiniti* was very close to the center of Bonhoeffer's thought:

"While other dialectical theologians thought of the sovereignty of revelation as gloriously manifest in its freedom and its intangibility, Bonhoeffer, quite after Lutheran fashion, thought of it as apparent in its self-disclosure. Bonhoeffer differed from the other dialectical theologians of those years in his emphasis on the *finitum capax infiniti*." "The Editing and Publishing of the Bonhoeffer Papers," *The Andover Newton Bulletin*, LII, No. 2 (December, 1959), p. 20. See also Bonhoeffer, *Gesammelte Schriften*, II (Munich: Kaiser Verlag, 1959), p. 278.

or later, and the whole house will feel it. This contemporary portrait of God is serving well at many points, but some leakage is beginning to be felt.

THE PROBLEM OF SUFFERING

I am convinced that the most serious leakage caused by this traditional and correct portrait of God today is at the point of the problem of suffering. There is something in this correct doctrine of God that keeps it from dealing responsibly with the problem, and therefore, because of this silence and carelessness, one can claim today that the problem of suffering has become a major barrier to faith for many sensitive unbelievers.[7]

It is not that the theology dominated by this doctrine of God does not mention the problem. It does, but when it does it is just not good enough. It may, for example, make much of the mystery of iniquity and ask us to shy away from questions about suffering on the grounds that we have no right to put impious questions to the holy God. It may speak of the ontological impossibility of evil; it may say that we are not asked to understand, but

---

[7] "The insurmountable barrier to Christianity does seem to me to be the problem of evil. But it is also a real obstacle for traditional humanism. There is the death of children, which means a divine reign of terror, but there is also the killing of children, which is an expression of a human reign of terror. We are wedged between two kinds of arbitrary law." Albert Camus, quoted by John Cruickshank, *Albert Camus and the Literature of Revolt* (New York: Galaxy Books, Oxford University Press, 1960), pp. xii-xiii.

only to fight evil; it may say that God is the source of all, good and evil alike, and this is what it means to affirm the divinity of God, and if we don't like it we don't need to affirm him.

Now this kind of evasion may be correct, may even be true, and is certainly very safe. But we miss something: we miss the curious fact that participation in the reality of suffering sometimes destroys the very possibility of faith. The special power of the problem of suffering is that it can really dry up in a man any capacity or wish to call out for the presence of God. If theology cannot reshape its statements about God to face this fact, many men will continue to prefer some sort of humanism without answers to a correct doctrine of God without answers. Leslie Fiedler has recently defined a position he calls "tragic humanism" which is really more sensitive to the power of suffering to hurt us than many theological answers. The tragic humanists assume, he writes,

> that the world of appearances is at once real and a mask through which we can dimly perceive more ultimate forces at work; that Nature is inscrutable, perhaps basically hostile to man, but certainly in some sense alien; that in man and Nature alike, there is a "diabolical" element, a "mystery of iniquity"; that it is impossible to know fully either God or ourselves, and that our only protection from destructive self-deceit is the pressure and presence of others; that to be alone, therefore, is to be lost; that evil is real, and that the thinking man breaks his heart trying to solve its compatibility with

the existence of a good God or his own glimmering perceptions of goodness.[8]

In spite of the quasi-theological language here, and in spite of the vivid description of what Christians would call man's ineradicable sinfulness, this is not a point of view that can be yoked together with most traditional Christian affirmations. It is not God, but the "pressure and presence of others," that renders the darkness tolerable. The world can be related to goodness or to God only if one is willing to break one's heart in the attempt. There is something "out there," and there is no abiding reality here. The perception of tragedy does not lead to God (as in many conventional existentialist invitations to religion) but leads sadly away from him. Now this is not a position that can be assimilated by many of us, but it is a powerful and widespread position; indeed, in some ways, it is the most plausible available alternative to Christianity. And it may be better than much of what we call Christianity.

Here is an example of the power of suffering to destroy faith. A few days ago before his execution at the hands of the Gestapo for his role in the July 20, 1944, plot against Hitler's life, Dr. Carl Goerdeler wrote some

---

[8] *Op. cit.*, pp. 417-18. The quotation continues:

"From this it follows that the writer's duty is to say, 'Nay!': to deny the easy affirmations by which most men live, and to expose the blackness of life most men try deliberately to ignore. For tragic humanists, it is the function of art not to console or sustain, much less to entertain, but to *disturb* by telling a truth which is always unwelcome."

final words in his cell. Goerdeler was a product of the liberal Protestant culture of Germany at its highest. A devout Christian, a deep lover of his own nation, he early saw the threat of Hitler and worked as a leader in the resistance movement at unbelievable cost to his own security and safety. At the close of his life, his whole structure of belief fell into a heap at his feet as he meditated on the events he had known.

> Unable to sleep I have asked myself whether there is a God who is interested in the fate of the individual. I find it hard to believe so, for this God has permitted a few hundred thousand men bestialized, insane or blinded to drown mankind in rivers of blood and agony and crush it under mountains of horror and despair. He lets millions of decent people suffer and die without raising a finger. Is this justice? Is not this sort of collective punishment the very reverse of justice? What a botcher of a God who knows the wrongdoers and the apostates and punishes the upright and the faithful. No, it is inconceivable. . . . I wrestle with my conscience about this and this inner conflict brightens the walls of my tiny cell, fills this dreary space with visions of fantasy and of memory. . . . Like the Psalmist . . . I argue with God because I do not understand Him. "Whom He loves, He takes early to Himself." No, that is not comfort; it is intolerable.[9]

---

[9] These fragments may be found on pp. 309 and 310 of a recent biography of Goerdeler by Gerhard Ritter, *The German Resistance* (New York: F. A. Praeger, 1958).

This is a moving, and we might almost say naive, statement of the terrible problem of unjust or undeserved suffering. But just what can theology say to it? Have we not been too sophisticated to be able to listen to such a direct statement? Would we not ask him to reformulate his objection or to take the long view or to remember the cross, or some other such facile piety? No one argued Goerdeler out of his faith. It simply became, at the end, impossible for him to live with. He died, apparently feeling abandoned by God, and at the end called to Christ for a God that had left him. "And still I seek through Christ this merciful God. I have not found him. O Christ, where lies the truth, where is the consolation?" [10]

Here is a man who lived in depths few of us have touched. Out of those depths he cried, and no answer came. The terrible problem did not receive a Christian answer, for the problem itself drove the Christian possibility quite away. We would do well to be careful in using the approach to Christian apologetics that seeks to place men in extreme situations of suffering or despair so that the impossible word of faith may be spoken. As Goerdeler reminds us, one of the things that these depths may do is destroy the capacity to receive that hoped-for answer. If we as Christians have never faced the burden of this problem, may it not be because we are afraid to make this effort of the imagination? Might we too not discover, with Goerdeler, that no answer would come

---

[10] *Ibid.,* p. 311.

back to us if we tried to cry out as passionately and naively as he did?

The classic passage in contemporary literature dealing with this issue is no doubt the dialogue between Father Paneloux and Dr. Rieux in Albert Camus' novel *The Plague*. Father Paneloux is the priest in Oran, which is suffering under bubonic plague. Rieux is a doctor, and both men have been struggling every waking hour to arrest the terror and death. When the plague began, Paneloux had delivered a sermon in the cathedral interpreting the plague, in rather traditional biblical terms, as a manifestation of God's judgment on the peoples' sins. But his confidence in this religious answer waned as he came to see the plague work its ravages on innocent and guilty, adult and child, believer and unbeliever. In this scene, the doctor and the priest have just witnessed the drawn-out and agonizing death of a child, and they are leaving the hospital together.

> Rieux swung round on him fiercely.
>
> "Ah, That child, anyhow, was innocent, and you know it as well as I do!"
>
> He strode on, brushing past Paneloux, and walked across the school playground. . . .
>
> He heard a voice behind him. "Why was there that anger in your voice just now? What we'd been seeing was as unbearable to me as it was to you!"
>
> Rieux turned toward Paneloux.
>
> "I know. I'm sorry. But weariness is a kind of madness. And there are times when the only feeling I have is one of mad revolt."

"I understand," Paneloux said in a low voice. "That sort of thing is revolting because it passes our human understanding. But perhaps we should love what we cannot understand."

Rieux straightened up slowly. He gazed at Paneloux, summoning to his gaze all the strength and fervor he could muster against his weariness. Then he shook his head.

"No, Father. I've a very different idea of love. And until my dying day I shall refuse to love a scheme of things in which children are put to torture."

A shade of disquietude crossed the priest's face. "Ah, doctor," he said sadly, "I've just realized what is meant by 'grace.' "

Rieux had sunk back on the bench. His lassitude had returned and from its depths he spoke, more gently:

"It's something I haven't got; that I know. But I'd rather not discuss that with you. We're working side by side for something that unites—beyond blasphemy and prayers. And it's the only thing that matters."

Paneloux sat down beside Rieux. It was obvious that he was deeply moved.

"Yes, yes," he said, "you, too, are working for man's salvation."

Rieux tried to smile.

"Salvation's much too big a word for me. I don't aim so high. I'm concerned with man's health; and for me his health comes first."

Paneloux seemed to hesitate. "Doctor—" he began, then fell silent. Down his face, too, sweat was trickling. Murmuring: "Good-by for the present," he rose. His eyes were moist. When he turned to go, Rieux, who had seemed lost in thought, suddenly rose and took a step toward him.

"Again, please forgive me. I can promise there won't be another outburst of that kind."

Paneloux held out his hand, saying regretfully:

"And yet—I haven't convinced you!"

"What does it matter? What I hate is death and disease, as you well know. And whether you wish it or not, we're allies, facing them and fighting them together." Rieux was still holding Paneloux's hand. "So you see"—but he refrained from meeting the priest's eyes—"God himself can't part us now." [11]

What is there in this scene that compels us to stand with the doctor rather than with the priest? Is it Camus's greater sympathy with the doctor's views? Is it the slight touch of over-eager professionalism in the priest? Whatever the reason, the author has made it nearly impossible not to say that Rieux has a tenderness and honesty that the priest lacks.

But Camus does not stack his cards wholly in favor of the unbelieving doctor. This incident deeply affected Paneloux, and some time later he preached a second sermon in the cathedral. The narrator comments that Paneloux's style was now more gentle, his command of words

[11] Camus, *The Plague,* translated by Stuart Gilbert (New York: Alfred A. Knopf, 1957), pp. 196-97. This contemporary study of the relation between the saint and the rebel seems to bear some marks, even consciously borrowed ones, of the tavern scene between Alyosha and Ivan in *The Brothers Karamazov* (Penguin edition, pp. 276-88). The Dostoevsky chapter is entitled "Rebellion," and Rieux's expression of "mad revolt" is very close to Ivan's position.

less certain. He spoke of his people as "we" rather than "you," and the message of the plague as the judgment of God was quite absent. In this sermon, Paneloux declared that nothing was more important than a child's suffering, and that there were no answers to such a problem. We have our backs against the wall, and there are no simple devices by which that wall can be scaled. He refused to claim that the child's suffering would be matched by an eternity of bliss; besides, who could say that even endless bliss could compensate for a moment of suffering here? His decisive answer came in two passages:

> No, he, Father Paneloux, would keep faith with that tortured body on the Cross; he would stand fast, his back to the wall, and face honestly the terrible problem of a child's agony. And he would boldly say to those who listened to his words today: "My brothers, a time of testing has come for us all. We must believe everything or deny everything. And who among you, I ask, would dare to deny everything?" [12]

The priest ran a considerable risk. The suffering of a child could not be reconciled to anything we know about God. It forced us to the wall, without an answer. But, he asked, do we dare to give up our faith in God because of this? Rieux would answer, "Yes, we must." Later, as he approached his conclusion, Paneloux ran an even greater risk. He came close to the suggestion that faith in

------

[12] *Op. cit.*, p. 202.

God could not now be grasped clearly at all, that it will become clear only when this world passes away.

> "My brothers ... the love of God is a hard love. It demands total self-surrender, disdain of our human personality. And yet it alone can reconcile us to suffering and the deaths of children, it alone can justify them, since we cannot understand them, and we can only make God's will ours. That is the hard lesson I would share with you today. That is the faith, cruel in men's eyes, and crucial in God's, which we must ever strive to compass. We must aspire beyond ourselves toward that high and fearful vision. And on that lofty plane all will fall into place, all discords be resolved, and truth flash forth from the dark cloud of seeming injustice.[13]

Here Paneloux is saying that faith is not something we have, but something we hope for; that faith is promise or hope—an eschatological, not a present, reality. The single thing that keeps Paneloux, we may say, from turning away from the discomfort of such a faith altogether, as Rieux rather sadly has done, is the tortured body of Christ on the cross. This is no answer to a child's suffering, but a recognition that we must live with such injustice as our normal lot in this life. In these passages, at least, Paneloux's faith is very close to the edge of unfaith, and the gulf we felt between Rieux and Paneloux in their earlier conversations seems very greatly reduced.

In these passages, Camus has not only laid bare the real terror of the problem of suffering, he has offered some

---

[13] *Ibid.*, pp. 205-6.

profound suggestions for the Christian who is dissatisfied with no answer and with easy answers. But "the divinity of God" is not the basis of his answer at all. God as holy judge was the answer in the earlier sermon; but in the final words it is God's hard love as shown through the tortured body on the cross. It may be that Father Paneloux's theology is inadequate. But something can be said for the point that it is a good deal more satisfactory than the attempts to face the problem in terms of the classical portrait of God we sketched out earlier in this chapter.[14]

This is the point. The experiences of many men in our time have suggested that the traditional sovereign and omnipotent God is a difficult God to perceive or to meet. In place of this God, the impotent God, suffering with men, seems to be emerging. In a familiar passage, Bonhoeffer has described such a suffering God:

> So our coming of age forces us to a true recognition of our situation *vis à vis* God. God is teaching us that we must live as men who can get along very well with-

---

[14] Archibald MacLeish's play *J.B.* (Boston: Houghton Mifflin Co., 1957) raises, with far less subtlety than *The Plague*, some of the same issues. MacLeish, like Camus, protests against the coldness and indifference of what he takes to be the biblical God (p. 95). There is also the feeling that no traditional view of God can face honestly the dreadful reality of human suffering. And there are also, quite hidden and apparently of little interest to the author, one or two suggestions that remind us a little of Father Paneloux's final sermon. These are the references to the weakness of God (pp. 50, 89) and to the idea of God's needing to be forgiven (pp. 138, 140). MacLeish does not use, in his climactic scene, this image of the weak God. If he had, it might have made for a more interesting solution than the love-affirming, God-denying one he actually set down.

> out him. The God who is with us is the God who for-
> sakes us. . . . The God who makes us live in this world
> without using him as a working hypothesis is the God
> before whom we are ever standing. Before God and
> with him we live without God. God allows himself to
> be edged out of the world, and that is exactly the way,
> the only way, in which he can be with us and help us.[15]

Thus, while we wait to see whether we can really abide
the appearance of this weak God, we begin to suspect that
the other God, the God of the Augustinian-Reformed
tradition, is not only remote, he is irrelevant; he not only
is far from us, he has departed from us. It is a very short
step, but a critical one, to move from the otherness of
God to the absence of God. But this is what the problem
of suffering tempts some to do. Many are saying, not out
of confidence or pride, but out of a kind of exhausted
sadness, much like that of Dr. Rieux, "perhaps this other
God is not." How can we estimate this experience of the
disappearance of the traditional God from the world?

THE DEATH OF GOD

I am not here referring to a belief in the non-existence
of God.[16] I am talking about a growing sense, in both

---

[15] *Letters and Papers from Prison*, pp. 163-64.

[16] "The world has become an entity rounded off in itself, which is
neither actually open at certain points where it merges into God, nor
undergoes at certain observable points the causal impact of God . . .
but it points to God as its presupposition only as a whole, and even
so not very obviously. . . . We are experiencing today that we can
make no image of God that is not carved from the wood of this

non-Christians and Christians, that God has withdrawn, that he is absent, even that he is somehow dead. Elijah taunted the false prophets and suggested that their god may have gone on a journey, since he could not be made to respond to their prayers (I Kings 18:27). Now, many seem to be standing with the false prophets, wondering if the true God has not withdrawn himself from his people. This feeling ranges from a sturdy unbelieving confidence in God's demise to the troubled believer's cry that he is no longer in a place where we can call upon him. Arthur Koestler represents the confident mood:

> God is dethroned; and although the incognisant masses are tardy in realising the event, they feel the icy draught caused by that vacancy. Man enters upon a spiritual ice age; the established churches can no longer provide more than Eskimo huts where their shivering flock huddles together.[17]

The patronizing and confident tone of this announcement reminds us of both Feuerbach and Nietzsche. In the

---

world. The educated man of our time has the duty, painful though fruitful, to accept this experience. He is not to suppress it by a facile, anthropomorphic 'belief in God,' but interpret it correctly, realizing that, in fact, it has nothing in common with atheism." Karl Rahner, "Wissenschaft als Confession?" *Wort und Wahrheit*, November, 1954, pp. 812-3. Quoted by Hans Urs von Balthasar, *Science, Religion and Christianity* (London: Burns & Oates, 1958), p. 95. Published in America by The Newman Press, Westminster, Md.

[17] "The Trail of the Dinosaur," *Encounter* (London), May, 1955. One should add that Koestler never seems to stand still, and that at the close of his recent book *The Lotus and the Robot* (London: Hutchinson & Co., Ltd., 1960), he has a very modest word of praise for Christianity, and, if not for dogma, at least for "the tenets of Judeo-Christian ethics."

famous passage in "The Gay Science" where the idea of the death of God is put forward by Nietzsche, a madman is portrayed as searching for God, calling out for him, and finally concluding that he and all men have killed him. The man's hearers do not understand his words, and he concludes that he has come with his message too early. He goes on to wander about the city's churches, calling out, "What are these churches now if they are not the tombs and sepulchers of God?" Koestler's igloos and Nietzsche's tombs are spiritually, if not architecturally, related. But in spite of Nietzsche's statement that the madman had come too soon, his declaration of God's death was heard and believed. And in the nineteenth century, as DeLubac writes, "man is getting rid of God in order to regain possession of the human greatness which, it seems to him, is being unwarrantably withheld by another. In God he is overthrowing an obstacle in order to gain his freedom." [18] Freud shared something of this Nietzschean conviction that God must be dethroned and killed to make way for the proper evaluation and freedom of man. And of course, as against many forms of religion, even this strident cry bears some truth.

But Koestler's confident assurance of God's dethronement and death is not the only way modern man describes his sense of God's absence or disappearance. When Dr. Tillich refers to the death of God he usually means the abolition of the idea of God as one piece of being alongside others, of God as a big person. Death of God for

---

[18] *Op. cit.*, p. 6.

him is thus the death of the idols, or the false gods. The novels of Albert Camus, on the other hand, portray not only a world from which the false gods, and the holy God of the theological revival, have departed, but a world from which any and all gods have silently withdrawn. The world of these novels is a world in which the word God simply refuses to have any meaning. This is not treated as a good thing or a terrible thing; it is just a fact that is ruefully assumed. It is the God described by the best and most sophisticated theologians of our time, who seems to many today to have withdrawn from his world. When we feel this, we do not feel free or strong, but weak, unprotected, and frightened.[19]

We seem to be those who are trying to believe in a time of the death of God. Just what do we mean when we say this? We mean that the Augustinian-Reformed portrait of God itself is a picture of a God we find more and more elusive, less and less for us or with us. And so we wonder if God himself is not absent. When we speak of the death of God, we speak not only of the death of the idols or the falsely objectivized Being in the sky; we speak, as well, of the death in us of any power to affirm any of the traditional images of God. We mean that the

---

[19] "Men are frightened at the absence of God from the world, they feel that they can no longer realize the Divine, they are terrified at God's silence, at his withdrawal into his own inaccessibility.... This experience which men think they must interpret theoretically as atheism, is yet a genuine experience of the most profound existence ... with which popular Christian thought and speech will not have finished for a long time." Rahner, *op. cit.*, p. 812, quoted by Von Balthasar, *op. cit.*, p. 96.

world is not God and that it does not point to God.[20]
Since the supports men have always depended on to help
them affirm God seem to be gone, little wonder that
many take the next step and wonder whether God himself has gone. Little wonder that Lent is the only season
when we are at home, and that that cry of dereliction
from the cross is sometimes the only biblical word that
can speak to us. If Jesus can wonder about being for-
saken by God, are we to be blamed if we wonder?

BEYOND THE DEATH OF GOD

Now, a believing Christian can face without distress
any announcement about the disappearance of the idols
from the religious world of men, but he cannot live as a
Christian for long with the suspicion that God himself
has withdrawn. How is it possible to turn this difficult
corner, and to move from an acknowledgment of God's
disappearance to a sense of some kind of reappearance

---

[20] The classical Reformation conception of Providence depended
for its formulation on the presence of a whole series of orders that
were self-evident to sixteenth-century man: the order of the celestial
bodies, the order of the political realm, the order and predictability of
the natural world, the order and inner coherence of the self. Men as
diverse as Calvin and Shakespeare drew on this experience of order
in their own work. In the *Institutes*, I. 5., Calvin used this external
orderliness as a means of illuminating the sovereign care of God over
the world. Tragedy, for Shakespeare, was the unusual and odd breakdown of the natural order of human life. Hamlet's perception that
"the time is out of joint" is a perception of a disorder that is the basis
of Shakespeare's sense of tragedy. See also Ulysses' speech on order
in *Troilus and Cressida*, Act I, Scene 3.

and presence? This sense of the separation of God from the world, Ronald Gregor Smith writes,

> does not lead to mere or sheer undialectical atheism. Any assertion of the absence of God and even further of his non-existence among the phenomena of the world is dialectically confronted by the equal assertion of his presence. I am sorry if this sounds like a mere verbal trick, but it cannot be helped.[21]

There is something disarming about Gregor Smith's unwillingness to look carefully at the connections between the sense of disappearance of God and the problem of his reappearance. But his way of putting it does indeed sound like a verbal trick, and we must try to discover if there are not ways of moving from the one state to the other.

One of the favorite contemporary attempts to do this might be called the Augustinian doubt maneuver. Augustine noted that he overcame his temptation toward skepticism by observing that even skepticism implied some affirmation of truth, the truth at least of the skeptical position.

> Everyone who knows that he is in doubt about something, knows a truth, and in regard to this that he knows he is certain. Therefore he is certain about a truth. Consequently everyone who doubts if there be

---

[21] "A Theological Perspective of the Secular," *The Christian Scholar,* XLIII, No. 1 (March, 1960), p. 22.

a truth has in himself a true thing on which he does not doubt.[22]

This may or may not be a convincing way to overcome radical skepticism. But it certainly cannot be used to mean that we can, by a kind of interior maneuver, affirm that we know the very thing we doubt. Augustine did not use it thus; we may doubt one truth, but that implies, he tells us, that we know another thing in our act of doubt, namely, that we are doubters. But some Christians have tried to claim that somehow doubt implies faith. God's existence, we are often told, is most profoundly proven in the very experience of doubting or denying him. Of course, passionate doubt has a resemblance to passionate faith. Both have a deep concern for the problem of truth; both real doubt and real faith deeply care. But it is not good enough to suggest that "There is no God" or "I cannot know that there is a God" really bears the same meaning as "Thou art my God." Let us continue to say that doubt is a necessary way for many of us to faith; that faith never overcomes doubt finally and completely; that lively faith can bear a good deal of doubt around the edges. But the depth of doubt is not the depth of faith; these are two places, not one, and a choice must finally be made between them. We cannot evade such a problem by a trick of redefinition.

This confusion of doubt and faith obscures the problem of moving from an affirmation about the disappear-

---

[22] *On True Religion*, XXIX. 73.

ance of God to an affirmation of his presence. I wonder if the following, and quite beautiful, passage from Dr. Tillich, is not also obscure in its apparent identification of having with not-having.

> To the man who longs for God and cannot find Him; to the man who wants to be acknowledged by God and cannot even believe that He is; to the man who is striving for a new and imperishable meaning of his life and cannot discover it—to this man Paul speaks. We are each such a man. Just in this situation, where the Spirit is far from our consciousness, where we are unable to pray or to experience any meaning in life, the Spirit is working quietly in the depth of our souls. In the moment when we feel separated from God, meaningless in our lives, and condemned to despair, we are not left alone. The Spirit, sighing and longing in us and with us, represents us. It manifests what we really are. In feeling this against feeling, in believing this against belief, in knowing this against knowledge, we like Paul, possess all.[23]

Now this is less specious than the doubt-equals-faith position. And it points to a profound truth. Faith is never the claim to own or possess. God comes to us finally when we confess that we have nothing in our hands to bring. Our not-knowing alone leads to knowing; our not-having is the only way to possession. All this is true, and very close to the Protestant conviction that God's

---

[23] *The Shaking of the Foundations* (New York: Charles Scribner's Sons, 1948), p. 139.

is to sinners and not to saints. But it will not do.
word as Dr. Tillich's can do much. It can per-
he man who struggles for God that there is a sense
h he has been found. It can portray the Christian
on attractively as one which knows, welcomes, and
with the experience of struggle and not-knowing.
will not serve to transform an experience of not-
g into an experience of having. For all of our ver-
balizing, these remain two different experiences, and we
are not finally helped by those who do not face openly
the distinctions.

The curious thing about this matter of God's disappearance is that even in those moments when we are
most keenly aware of God's absence we still, somehow,
find it possible to pray for his return. Perhaps we ought
to conclude that the special Christian burden of our time
is the situation of being without God. There is, for some
reason, no possession of God for us, but only a hope,
only a waiting.[24] This is perhaps part of the truth: to be

---

[24] Perhaps one of the reasons why Samuel Beckett's *Waiting for Godot* has fascinated us is that Beckett has portrayed so many of the ambiguities in our feeling about God today. Godot, for whom Vladimir and Estragon wait, seems to stand for the traditional God for whom all of us think we are waiting. This Godot has a white beard (p. 59), he punishes those who reject him (p. 60), he saves (pp. 48, 61), he is the one to whom Vladimir and Estragon offer a "kind of prayer," a "vague supplication" (p. 13). In Godot there is a combi-nation of absence and harshness. He is always postponing his visit; yet he is said to beat the young boy's brother (p. 34). Vladimir asks the boy, Godot's messenger, "What does he do, Mr. Godot?" And the boy replies, "He does nothing, Sir" (p. 59). At the close of the play, when Godot still has not arrived, Estragon asks if they should not drop Godot altogether. To this Vladimir replies, "He'd punish us" (p. 60). Finally, is the Christian critic being over-eager when he

a Christian today is to stand, somehow, as a man w
God but with hope. We know too little to know
now; we only know enough to be able to say th
will come, in his own time, to the broken and c
heart, if we continue to offer that to him. Faith
many of us, we might say, purely eschatological.
kind of trust that one day he will no longer be a
from us. Faith is a cry to the absent God; faith is i

An identification of faith with hope is possible, but a
little more can be said. The absent one has a kind of
presence; the one for whom the Christian man waits still
makes an impact on us. W. H. Auden has described this
presence very accurately.

> In our anguish we struggle
> To elude Him, to lie to Him, yet His love observes
> His appalling promise; His predilection
> As we wander and weep is with us to the end.
> Minding our meanings, our least matter dear to Him. . . .
> It is where we are wounded that is when He speaks
> Our creaturely cry, concluding His children
> In their mad unbelief to have mercy on them all
> As they wait unawares for His world to come.[25]

In this there is waiting, but also something else. God is
also the one whom we struggle to elude; as Augustine
says, "Thou never departest from us, and yet only with

---

notes that the waiting takes place by a tree—the only part of the land-
scape that has not died (pp. 60-1)? (The page references are to the
Grove Press edition, New York, 1954.)

[25] From *The Age of Anxiety*, by W. H. Auden. Copyright 1946,
1947 by W. H. Auden. Reprinted by permission of Random House, Inc.

difficulty do we return to thee." [26] He speaks to us at the point where we are wounded. And even though our wound is our separation from him, the separation is not absolute. The reflections of Psalm 139 and Genesis 32: 24-25 in this fragment from Auden remind us of part of our situation.

Thus, neither "death of God," "absence of God," nor "disappearance of God" is wholly adequate to describe the full meaning of our religious situation. Our experience of God is deeply dissatisfying to us, even when we are believers. In one sense God seems to have withdrawn from the world and its sufferings, and this leads us to accuse him of either irrelevance or cruelty. But in another sense, he is experienced as a pressure and a wounding from which we would love to be free. For many of us who call ourselves Christians, therefore, believing in the time of the "death of God" means that he is there when we do not want him, in ways we do not want him, and he is not there when we do want him.

The rediscovery of the divinity of God which we described at the start of this chapter seems defective on two counts. It gives us a portrait of God that does not seem able to receive honestly the threat posed by the problem of suffering, and it does not accurately enough describe the curious mixture of the disappearance and presence of God that is felt by many today. I am not sure just what ought to be our proper response to this curious mixture. There seems to be some ground for terror here, so that

---

[26] *Confessions* VIII. 8.

we can partly agree with Ingmar Bergmann when he said recently that "if God is not there, life is an outrageous terror." [27] Yet in another sense we face the special texture of our unsatisfactory religious situation with calmness. Most of us are learning to accept these things: the disappearance of God from the world, the coming of age of the world, as it has been called, the disappearance of religion as a lively factor in modern life, the fact that there are men who can live both without God and without despair. We are coming to accept these calmly as events not without their advantages. Perhaps our calmness will disappear when we face the possibility that God will even more decisively withdraw—that he will withdraw from our selves as he has already withdrawn from the world, that not only has the world become sheer world but that self will become sheer self. For if there are men today who can do without God, it still seems to be true that we cannot do so. We are afraid of ourselves without him, even though what we know of him may be only a pressure and a wounding.

Finally, this portrait of the situation between man and God today, in the time (as we have called it) of the death of God, is not satisfactory if this is all we know. We have really described a bondage, not a freedom; a disturbance and very little else. If this were all there were to the Christian faith, it would not be hard to reject it. Is there, then, a deliverance from this absent-present disturber God? There is, and the deliverance will

---

[27] *Time*, March 14, 1960, p. 66.

somehow be connected with another image of God—
what we have already referred to as the impotent God
—that emerges when we try to take our next step and
say something about Jesus the Lord.[28] But I have not
stated, and I do not want to state, that we can know
nothing of God apart from Jesus. We can and do know
something, and it is just this unsatisfactory mixture of his
presence and absence, his disturbance.[29] As we move to-

---

[28] In a recent debate on the BBC, Professor Gregor Smith tried to
bring together the sense of the disappearance of God from the world
and a Christian affirmation about Jesus.

"I recognize in that situation that you describe, for yourself and
for us all, what you might call the reappearance of God, a veiled
reappearance certainly, and I should focus this in the life of Christ,
in his life of being for other people, which is how you can sum it up
—just being for other people absolutely. I should focus it there, and
also in the constellation of events that gather round that particular
bit of human history both before and after. I find it almost impossible to say more than this, just because I recognize at once that
though I see here action of God, it is, of course, ambiguous. It is still
possible to say: 'Well, I just don't see it.'" *The Listener* (London)
January 21, 1960.

[29] At this point the Jew—both ancient Israel and the modern Jew
—becomes significant for Christian theological reflection. Jewish existence is an important part of the evidence we cite for our conviction
that God is the one who leaves us alone and the one who disturbs us.
The Jew is the one who knows what it is to be disturbed by both
God and men, and in this sense the Christian never ceases being a
Jew when he is a Christian. The reality and integrity of Jewish existence are what prevent the Christian from holding too rigid a Christological definition of God. "Apart from Christ I am an atheist" is
false; "apart from Christ I am a Jew" would be closer to the truth.
This close theological dependence of the Christian on the Jew (which
is a mutual dependence for some Jewish thinkers, but not for others)
is one reason why we ought to be deeply disturbed by the lack of
really effective theological conversation between Christianity and
Judaism today. It is arguable that there is more real theological affinity between Protestantism and some forms of Judaism than between

wards the center of the Christian faith, Jesus Christ, will we be able to overcome the instability of our belief in a time of the death of God or, even reckoning with Jesus, will something of this experience remain?

Protestantism and Roman Catholicism. The latter is a Christian heresy, whereas Judaism is in some way a theological necessity. The Protestant needs to learn what it means to stand with the Jew, even when the Jew is not willing to stand with him.

Chapter Three

CHAPTER 3

Jesus the Lord

If we are dealing with the divinity of Jesus we must speak especially of his weakness.—Bonhoeffer

Many consider it bad form today to hint, even dimly, that one can say anything about God apart from Jesus. Theology *is* Christology, and with Jesus we must begin. This is a tempting procedure that must be avoided. I have drawn a picture of man and God in our world today that seems to me to be true, at least for some of us. It is an unstable position, to be sure, but it does suggest that something about God's presence and absence can be affirmed without reference to Jesus.[1]

---

[1] In a recent article in *The Christian Century*, Professor H. Richard Niebuhr utters these words of complaint. "I wish to reject," he writes, "the tendency in much post-liberal theology to equate theology with Christology and to base on a few passages of the New Testament a new unitarianism of the second person of the Trinity. In my confession of faith, as in that of many men I know, the expression of trust in God and the vow of loyalty to him comes before the acknowledgement of Christ's lordship. I realize that it is not so for all

71

We do not come to Jesus, therefore, so that we may meet a God hitherto unknown. We come to Jesus because the God we have found apart from him is a kind of absentee enemy who does not make it possible for us either to think or to live as the Christians we wish to be.

THREE CHRISTOLOGICAL QUESTIONS

What we find in Jesus is determined largely by the questions we raise to which we suppose him to be the answer. There are perhaps three types of question that men put today to Jesus, or to themselves concerning Jesus. Each represents an interest in a different set of theological problems, yet all are important, all are needed for a good Christology, and we are not wholly free to attend only to one and reject the others. The first question concerns our knowledge of God. How dare we, it is asked, in a world in which the little knowledge we have is so hard to get clear, with minds trained to measure and verify, how dare we claim to know something so utterly beyond the observation of men as God appears to be? Can we know him at all? We have already partly asked this question, and heard something of an answer. It runs like this: of course you cannot know God if you

---

Christians but I protest against a dogmatic formulation that reads me and my companions out of the church." (Excerpt from "Reformation: Continuing Imperative," by H. Richard Niebuhr, March 2, 1960, p. 250).

This is a just complaint, though one wonders whether there is not a good deal more biblical evidence for the rejected position than the few New Testament passages Professor Niebuhr refers to.

continue to search for ways of verification like those you use for your knowledge of the external world. You cannot know him at all by argument, by inspection of nature, or by introspection. But he has revealed himself to you, and your task as a Christian is not to squint towards the heavens, but to point simply to the life and death of Jesus Christ. This is the way you answer when the question about the knowledge of God is raised.

This approach to Jesus is being used today whenever Christians are facing scientists or philosophers who challenge the ways of knowing that Christians use. In the contemporary conversations, for instance, between believers and analytical philosophers, the problem and the answer are generally set forth in some such way as this.

A second kind of question concerning Jesus begins not so much with the dilemma of not-knowing God, but with our experience of bondage and dismay when we are apart from God. Here the cry is not for knowledge, but for salvation. Apart from God, life seems a terror or a joke. We are a mystery to ourselves, an unlovely mystery we do not like, and we need to be freed from this unwilling bondage. We cannot perform this act of liberation, nor can our ideals or our culture. However we may flee to the plausible human structures available to us—work, love of beauty, the people we hold dear—we find the same thing. We can love and enjoy these things, but they cannot deliver us from ourselves, except for fleeting moments of ecstasy. When such moments are past, we are still the same selves in bondage to guilt and pride. What shall we do to be saved? And the Christian

response to this is familiar and true. You are free to do
everything that this world invites you to do except this
one thing: you are not free to save yourself. And for a
very simple reason. Salvation is from bondage to the self
—this is what you long to be freed from. And the self is
not able, by willing, to free the self. Such an act of the
will only further involves the self, and leads either to
self-congratulation when you seem to succeed or self-
hatred when you seem to fail. But when you come to see
that this is the one thing you cannot do, you are prepared to accept from God what he can do. He can free
you because he can and has forgiven you. And in the gift
of forgiveness that is ever offered to the truly broken
and contrite, the life of freedom you have looked for in
the wrong way is available to you. The New Testament
story of God acting in Jesus is primarily a story of your
life, in which forgiveness and freedom are offered to you.

This tradition might be styled the classical Protestant
one. In such terms as these, we try to make the basic
Protestant insight of justification by faith come alive.
There are a number of variations of it in our midst, and
the most interesting is the existentialist one. Here the
human problem is put in terms of meaninglessness. We
are not so much bound by our selfhood as aimlessly adrift
in a world to which no secure meanings can be attached.
Our dilemma is not too much self, but no authentic sense
of our own selfhood. Here, when the answer is formu-
lated, Jesus is not so much the place where the message
of forgiveness is uniquely spoken, but the logos, the
promise and reality of meaning in the midst of meaning-

lessness. God is sometimes defined in this tradition as the meaning of existence, and to be touched by him in Jesus is to be touched by a meaning not our own, but a meaning nonetheless in which we can live, and which enables us to make our way through a disordered world with courage and serenity.

A third type of question that is being put to Jesus today is not so theological or existential. It may be described as the question of the layman rather than the theologian, and thus it may be more important than the others. It is not a question about the knowledge of God; and it is not a question about salvation or about meaning in a meaningless world. It is a question about doing the will of God. In the modern world, which does not operate by doing the will of God, but in its own terms of power, achievement, and success, how can we do the will of God without destroying ourselves both professionally and personally?

The answer to this question is not an abstract conception like love or service or humility. It is concrete person Jesus Christ. He, and not some principle, is God's will.[2]

These are perhaps three of the basic ways that Christians find themselves coming to Jesus today. Each of them is a correct way, each asks a legitimate question, and each shapes an answer that makes some sense. It is

---

[2] "Proving what is God's will is possible only on the foundation of the knowledge of God's will in Jesus Christ. Only upon the foundation of Jesus Christ, only within the space which is defined by Jesus Christ, only 'in' Jesus Christ can man prove what is the will of God." Dietrich Bonhoeffer, *Ethics* (London: SCM Press, 1955), pp. 162-63. Published in the U. S. by Macmillan Co. (N. Y.).

not necessary for us to choose between them, however, and an attempt ought to be made to state what can be believed about Jesus in a way that would find some affinity with all three of these approaches. None of us can have anything like the whole truth, and even when we satisfy these three questions, a great deal will be left over.

The New Testament Struggle

If we are to find satisfactory answers to these questions, we have no choice but to turn to the New Testament record. It is not the case that we will be able automatically to affirm for ourselves what it says, but we cannot come to our own affirmations about Jesus without participating in its struggle to define and to describe Jesus' meaning. Our struggle depends on, but is not identical with, its struggle.

The New Testament struggle to understand who Jesus was and what he meant for the church can be seen as a struggle over the names and titles to be given him, and the names and titles, if any, that he allowed himself to be given. One of the first facts that strike us in the New Testament record is the extreme reticence Jesus had in accepting the traditional titles "Christ," "Son of God," "Son of man." Why was he so evasive? If he seemed to shy away from them, shouldn't we shy away ourselves? Jesus' reticence is explained, surely, by his desire to remove any possible barriers between men and a real meeting with God through his work and words. If some traditional title had been clearly affirmed, men might have confidently pigeonholed him, understood him, and left him alone. Because God was claiming men through his mission, he carefully removed all possibility of a simple definition of his work that might have led men to make their peace with him too readily.

Yet we cannot quite make our peace with the problem of Jesus' name by showing how he seemed to avoid all traditional names. We must enter into this form of the New Testament struggle by examining a few of the traditional titles, and by asking which of them, if any, can be used to help us formulate what we can know of Jesus today.

The New Testament itself reminds us that the Gospel is received by two quite distinct kinds of communities in the early period: the church in and around Palestine, centered in Jerusalem; and the church moving out from the holy land into the Graeco-Roman world. The theological needs of these two groups vary, and the titles for Jesus in the Palestinian church and in the churches of the Hellenistic world correspondingly vary. In the Palestinian church, the titles have as their function the description of Jesus' relationship to the Old Testament, particularly to the hope of the Messiah and the hope for the new age, anticipated in the Old Testament, and proclaimed as now present among men in Jesus. "Christ" is the chief title used here, and the Christians used the title referring to the long-awaited Messiah of the Old Testament to say that in Jesus the new age, the kingdom, the last days, are in the process of arriving.

Because the first task of the Jews who had become

followers of Jesus was to declare to their fellow Jews that their time of waiting was at an end, the statement that Jesus is the Messiah was a dominant note in their preaching. But a number of problems arise before we can be satisfied with the adequacy of the statement that Jesus is the Messiah. It is remarkable that "Christ" became the dominant title and even part of the proper name, for Jesus himself was particularly reserved about it, and it may be that he did not claim it for himself at all. "Messiah" bears many meanings in the Old Testament, and one of the most frequent is that of political ruler or king; a figure of power, overturning, at his coming, the enemies of the Jewish people. Jesus decisively rejected any political ambitions, as the temptation stories make clear. Perhaps he was drawn to this traditional political role; a man is not ordinarily tempted by something to which he is not powerfully drawn. But the temptation narratives suggest that Jesus considered the devil himself to be behind the political idea of messiahship. So there is, in the whole New Testament story, a secrecy, a reticence, even a rejection of this kind of messiahship: in Mark 14:61-2; 15:2 ff.; and especially the so-called confession of Peter at Caesarea Philippi, Mark 8:27 ff. This latter is really a story, not of what Peter discovered, but of the great gulf between Peter's understanding of what being the Christ-Messiah meant, and Jesus' understanding. Peter meant by Christ power and authority. Jesus spoke of the suffering of the Son of man; Peter said such a thing could not be; and Jesus bitterly rebuked him. Is it really accurate to say that Peter "confessed" Jesus as the Christ?

Now Jesus' meaning is intimately bound up with the Old Testament hope; the new community he gathers is clearly related to the older idea of a messianic community to be gathered at the time of the new age. But a more exact description of Jesus' relationship to the Old Testament might be this: in some ways, Jesus is what the Old Testament means by Israel, which must suffer and become the means for the redemption of all. And in some ways he is what the Old Testament means by God. He forgives sin, which God alone can do, and this is one of the decisive grounds for the Pharisees' very early suspicion of Jesus as a blasphemous claimant to the status of God, as in Mark 2:7.

This is why it is so imprecise, and even inaccurate, for us to say that Jesus is the Christ. He was and is what Israel had longed for in their recorded history; but he did not come in the form which they expected. Thus today when a Christian says that Jesus is the Christ, and a Jew says that the Messiah is yet to come, the first is not exactly affirming what the second denies. Our theological debates with Judaism need to remember this.

It was essential that Christ become a dominant title at the beginning, for the idea of fulfillment of the Old Testament was absolutely essential for the Christian's understanding of Jesus. Yet Jesus' own avoidance of the title might be recalled in our time, as we try to state the subtle connection between him and the Old Testament story in perhaps other terms. Jesus Christ has, of course, become his name today, but even so, the function that the second part of the name describes is both true and misleading.

The title "Son of God" is used in both the Palestinian and Hellenistic churches. Jesus does not describe himself as such, though in Mark we find the title being given by God at the baptism, we find it on the lips of the demoniacs from time to time, and perhaps we hear it from the centurion at the moment of Jesus' death. In the Old Testament, Son of God does not refer to participation in a divine nature or substance, but to a divine calling or obedience. Israel is called son in this sense, special groups with specific commissions from God can be sons of God, and perhaps the Messiah is also referred to as the Son of God. In the Hellenistic thought-world, the background is wholly different; a Jew hearing the title would call up quite a different series of images from those of a Greek-speaking Gentile. Hellenistic religion is full of sons of God, divine and semidivine beings, mythical offspring of unions between divine figures and mortals. And to be a son in this sense is to have something of the substance of God within you. Perhaps the expression "form of God," in Philippians 2:6, has some of this Hellenistic color.

In addition to these two biblical meanings of "Son of God" we have the technical trinitarian meaning of the phrase, developed in the church's fight against Arianism in the fourth century. Though this church language is sometimes attacked as "Hellenistic," the Nicene "Son of God" is by no means the same thing as Son of God in the older Hellenistic tradition. As a matter of fact, the phrase is used in the fourth century as part of the church's attack on the Hellenistic disintegration of the Gospel at the hands of the Arian heretics. So alongside the two biblical meanings of the phrase we must set this third: Son of God as referring to a pre-existent being or "person," not God himself, but equal in power of divinity of God, who becomes flesh in Jesus. Son of God in this latter sense is used to affirm what came to be called the divinity of Christ. The function of "Son of God" in the New Testament is a little different; it is more concerned with Jesus' function than with "divinity."

For these reasons, it is very difficult to say what it means to call Jesus the Son of God. He does not refer to himself as such, though of course he is aware of standing in a special filial relation to God. He says "Abba" to God, and his disciples are invited to say "Our Father." But for us today, "Son of God" is perhaps the least satisfactory traditional term partly because of this threefold level of meaning that it bears. It was an essential title for the church in its early attempts to relate Jesus to the Old Testament and to the Hellenistic world; and it was decisive for the anti-Arianism struggle. But it is not obviously useful for us today.

"Son of man" is the title most frequently appearing on Jesus' own lips. But what this means when Jesus uses it, what the writers of the gospels meant by it, whether they accurately recorded Jesus' use of it, whether Jesus' reference to the coming of the Son of man referred to himself or to another to come, and which Old Testament and Jewish uses of the phrase can usefully illuminate

Jesus' use—all these questions are hotly debated today by New Testament scholars. No general lines of agreement are evident, and no agreement is even likely.

The Son of man material in the New Testament falls into two distinct groups. One, which probably reflects the passage in Daniel 7:13, describes the coming of the Son of man in the future, a supernatural divine figure (see Mark 8:38; 14:62). The second refers to the lowliness, the humiliation, suffering, and rejection of the Son of man (see Mark 8:31; 10:45). The church came to interpret Jesus as Son of man in the first, exalted sense, but the material in the New Testament does not convince us that Jesus thought of himself thus. It is probable that the church applied the exalted Son of man idea to Jesus because it was convinced that he did see himself as the lowly, suffering Son of man in the second sense. If this is true [3] we can have some confidence in saying that Jesus' special sense of his own mission and meaning involved almost exclusively the themes of lowliness, humiliation, suffering, and death, and not power or authority in the ordinary senses at all.

To say this, however, brings us to the final title we need to examine, the title "Lord." If Jesus' own self-awareness is one of impotence and suffering, how can the

---

[3] Dr. Eduard Schweizer, of Zurich, has stated this position with persuasive clarity. See his articles: "The Disciples of Jesus and the Post-Resurrection Church," *Union Seminary Quarterly Review*, May, 1960, pp. 282-83; and "The Son of Man," *Journal of Biblical Literature*, June, 1960, pp. 119-29; and his book *Lordship and Discipleship* (Studies in Biblical Theology) (London: SCM Press, 1960), especially p. 41.

idea of his being "the Lord" be maintained? To dare to describe Jesus' meaning for men as "Lord" involves an almost incredible assertion, both for a Jew trained in the Old Testament and for a Gentile from the wider Hellenistic world. Why incredible? Because the word "Lord" (*kyrios* in Greek) would bear a very precise meaning for a Jew who had learned his Old Testament in the Greek version. *Kyrios* in the Greek version of the Old Testament is used for the name of God himself; indeed, it is used there to translate several of the divine names of the Old Testament. And in the Jewish liturgies of the time, both in Palestine and in the Jewish communities in dispersion, *kyrios* is the common word referring to God. A Jew, therefore, looking at the Christian's claims for Jesus, will interpret the affirmation that Jesus is Lord to mean that Jesus is for the Christian what God himself is for the Jew.

In the Hellenistic world, which did not necessarily know the Greek Old Testament, the word Lord (*kyrios*) had a different meaning, but still a meaning difficult to relate to the lowliness of Jesus. In the Oriental and Hellenistic religions which filled the Roman Empire at the time of the beginning of the Christian movement, lordship—whether ascribed to a god or to a ruler—meant one thing: absolute power, deity, authority. Whatever you called *kyrios*-lord was what you owed absolute allegiance to, and there is good evidence that one of the reasons the confession of Jesus as Lord took such firm hold is that it served very clearly to state that a Christian can have no other lords, *kyrioi,* and especially cannot ascribe to the emperor the attribute of lordship-divinity that he claimed. The Christians were killed in the persecutions not because of their politics, but because to accept the emperor on his terms meant that there could be more than one absolute loyalty, more than one historic bearer of divine sovereignty, and this the Christian knew to be false, if he knew nothing else.

And yet, against this background of meaning, the earliest attempts to sum up the essence of Christian allegiance are almost certainly those confessions that state that Jesus is Lord, the only Lord. The lowly one who suffered and died: he is in fact what lordship means. We can see how this worked out by looking at what is one of the oldest pieces of material describing Jesus' meaning that we have preserved in the New Testament, the hymn Paul quotes in Philippians 2:6-11. Paul speaks of Christ Jesus,

> who, though he was in the form of God, did not count equality with God a thing to be grasped, but emptied himself, taking the form of a servant, being born in the likeness of men. And being found in human form he humbled himself and became obedient unto death, even death on a cross. Therefore God has highly exalted him and bestowed on him the name which is above every name, that at the name of Jesus every knee should bow, in heaven and on earth and under the earth, and every tongue confess that Jesus Christ is Lord, to the glory of God the Father.

Here is the church, wrestling with the fact of Jesus' earthly humiliation, yet daring to say that in this very lowliness he is the Lord. The idea of the pre-existence is clearly in evidence here, though it is not quite clear how, or in what form, Jesus is said to exist before his earthly life in the form of God. But the use of the idea of pre-existence is quite clear. In this passage, it means that when a disciple was called by the man Jesus "he had already met God himself in this calling." [4] In the form of the humble servant God himself is present, and therefore the one decisive name by which this Jesus is to be known is Lord, which is to say either to a Greek or to a Jew, the one through whom God meets you. In this way the church wrestled with the tension between power and weakness, between divinity and lowly, suffering humanity. "You know," Paul writes (2 Cor. 8:9), "the grace of our Lord Jesus Christ, that though he was rich" (with all the riches of God, "the form of God," as Paul puts it in his Philippian letter), "yet for your sake he became poor, so that by his poverty you might become rich"— not that we might become divine, but that we might know and meet God.

The idea of lordship contains another tension besides this one of exaltation and lowliness. It is the tension between presence and absence—Jesus with us over against Jesus as coming. After the resurrection, the church affirmed Jesus as the present Lord, but also as the one for whom they were waiting. The idea of the second coming has many meanings to it, but one thing it served to point out was that Jesus' lordship is not yet fully achieved, re-

---

[4] E. Schweizer, *Lordship and Discipleship*, p. 64.

vealed or complete. Paul can say (2 Cor. 5:6) that "while we are at home in the body we are away from the Lord." This sense of living, yet not living, in the final age of history is nicely described by an early prayer that has come down to us in the original Aramaic tongue, the liturgical expression, *maranatha*—Our Lord, come (see 1 Cor. 16:22 and Didache 10:6). This means, in part, "Come now to us in our worship of thee and be present in our midst." But it can also mean, and probably is intended to mean, "Come Lord in thy final power at the end of time." The early Christian summed up this double tension in which he lived by confessing Jesus as Lord: the crucified one is the one who brings us God; yet the present Lord is absent from us, and in the age to come we will yet see him and know his lordship more clearly than we ever can in this age.

The church, thus, gives the name of Lord to the lowly and humiliated one who was killed on a cross. In so doing, it has proposed the most radical revision of conventional ideas of divinity that can be imagined. Christianity's real contribution is this: when asked what it means by God, it points to the cross. Jesus is Lord by being a servant; to be Lord and to be servant are the same. He exercises his divinity and his sovereign power from the cross. Every subsequent placing of Christianity within the class of religions, every Christian speculation on what power and authority mean when applied to God, must reckon with this revolution. Both in the temptations and at Gethsemane (Matt. 26:52-3), Jesus is free to make use of what the world calls power and authority, and he refuses.

It is interesting, if not of decisive theological importance, to point out that this theme of the weakness of Jesus has exercised a curious fascination for some of the writers of our time.[5] The figure of Jesus in the Grand Inquisitor legend in Dostoevsky's *The Brothers Karamazov* is not only silent before the cardinal's monologue; his whole bearing is one of impotence and weakness.

---

[5] In the literature of the beat movement, the representatives have sometimes imposed their own alienation onto Jesus, and a peculiar kind of impotent redeemer is portrayed. One finds this occasionally in the novels, and most interestingly in a poem by Lawrence Ferlinghetti:

> You're hot they tell him
> and they cool him
> they stretch him on the Tree to cool
> and everybody after that is always making models
> of this tree with Him hung up
> and always crooning His name
> and calling Him to come down
> and sit in on their combo
> as if he is the king cat who's got to blow
> or they can't quite make it
>
> Only he don't come down from his tree
> Him just hang there on his tree
> looking real Petered out
> and real cool
>   and also
> according to a roundup
>   of late world news
> from the usual unreliable sources
>   real dead.

From *A Coney Island of the Mind* (New York: New Directions Books, 1958), 5.

Melville's *Billy Budd*, a work almost exactly contemporary with the Dostoevsky work, may be interpreted as a study of imperfect innocence, more permanent and enduring than the religion and the justice of men.

In our own time, the list of novels dealing with the weak or flawed Christ-like figure is an extensive one: Lawrence's *The Man Who Died*; Spina in Silone's *Bread and Wine*; *Miss Lonelyhearts*, by Nathaniel West; the corporal in Faulkner's *A Fable*; the description of Christ given by Jean-Baptiste at the end of Camus' *The Fall*.

The theme of the impotent and suffering Christ plays an important minor role in the poetry of Dylan Thomas:

> You who bow down at cross and altar
> Remember me and pity Him
> Who took my flesh and bone for armour
> And doublecrossed by mother's womb.
>
> ("Before I Knocked")

> In the name of the wanton
> Lost on the unchristened mountain
> In the center of dark I pray him
> That he let the dead lie though they moan
> For his briared hands to hoist them
> To the shrine of his world's wound....
>
> ("Vision and Prayer") [6]

To sum up this section: it can be claimed that one basic New Testament approach to the meaning of Jesus sees him as the humiliated and suffering Lord. The New Testa-

---

[6] These passages may be found on pp. 8 and 161-62 of *The Collected Poems of Dylan Thomas* (New York: New Directions, 1957).

ment, of course, says a good deal more than this, but those who cannot yet say this "more" with conviction can have a good conscience about saying this in faithfulness to the record. Let us turn again to the three "questions" we raised earlier in the chapter, and consider them in the light of this understanding of lordship.

LORDSHIP AS HUMILIATION ANSWERS THE QUESTIONS

Jesus and the knowledge of God. If one begins his reflections on this problem with the statement that Jesus is Lord, a first consequence may be some uneasiness with the formula "divinity of Christ," though not with the meaning behind the formula. Uneasiness, not because the phrase points to something false, but rather because it seems difficult to understand how either an affirmation or denial of it could make any sense. Let us assume you are asked, "Do you believe in the divinity of Christ?" It makes no difference whether the questioner is impeccably orthodox and suspects you are not, or wildly unitarian and suspects you of dogmatism. The question implies a comparison between two clearly known categories: one, called the divine or divinity; the other, the man Jesus. And the questioner wishes to know whether or not you find these two known categories commensurable. But the point is this: we do not have two known categories at all. We have Jesus the man. Of him we know something; not enough to satisfy, not enough to provide answers to our ethical problems, but enough to

be able to say what was characteristic of him and his way
with men. And we have further a decision of faith that
Jesus is the Lord, the one through whom God meets us.
But we do not know any separate category of divinity,
a separate divine essence by means of which we can define Jesus.[7] In the previous chapter, we described man's
situation before God today, and what we found there
was a "divinity" quite perplexing, dissatisfying, even
intolerable. That kind of divinity was both an absence
and a wounding presence: an absence or disappearance
from the world, and a pressure or presence in the heart
of the individual. In this sense, Jesus is not divine; as the
suffering Lord he is a protest against this kind of divinity, or, in better terms, he is a correction and a transfor-
mation of divinity as seen in that way.

If there is divinity apart from Jesus, it is a form of
divinity that Jesus as suffering Lord corrects, destroys,
transforms. In Jesus the Lord we see for the first time
what Christian "divinity" must be taken to be: it is God
withdrawing from all claims to power and authority and
sovereignty, and consenting to become himself the victim and subject of all that the world can do. The af-

---

[7] "Jesus Christ . . . is not God in a self-evident and explainable manner, but only in faith. This divine being does not exist. If Jesus Christ
is to be described as God, then one must not speak about his divine
essence, his omnipotence or his omniscience, but only about this weak
man among sinners, about his cradle and his cross. If we are dealing
with the divinity of Jesus we must speak especially of his weakness."
From a reconstructed version of Bonhoeffer's 1933 Berlin lectures on
Christology, *Gesammelte Schriften*, Vol. 3 (Munich: Kaiser Verlag,
1960), p. 233. Compare the passage from *Letters and Papers from
Prison*, pp. 163-64, quoted above, pp. 54-5.

flicting God of our previous chapter becomes now the afflicted God. Divinity in Jesus is not withdrawal from the world; it is a full consent to abide in the world, and to allow the world to have its way with it.

This is why we can't be content with the traditional way of formulating the question of the divinity of Jesus. "Divinity, divine essence?" we say. "Yes, we know a little of what this means, and what we know of it haunts and disturbs us, both because of its abdication from the world and because of its wounding presence in our hearts. But what we know of it by itself leads us to reject it, not to welcome it at all. In Jesus the Lord, the whole meaning of what it is to be God is so radically transformed that we can no longer move from divinity to Jesus (and thus to assert the divinity of Christ) but from Jesus to divinity, and to affirm that our picture of God is ultimately determined by seeing him as the one who has come in the lowliness of Jesus the Lord."

If it is true that "Luther limited our knowledge of God to our individual experience of temptation and our identification in prayer with the passion of God's son," [8] then there are some affinities between our position here and Luther's. God himself, Luther would say, is the remote one who comes to us directly only as law and demand. This is the terrible God whom man cannot abide or compass, for he is hidden from man's knowing. But, Luther went on, God has made himself small, and

---

[8] Erik H. Erikson, *Young Man Luther* (New York: W. W. Norton & Co., 1958), p. 253.

has willed to enter wholly into the lives of men in the humanity of Jesus. Here he is not hidden; he is manifest. Here the infinite one has put himself completely into the finite space of Jesus the man.

Two passages, characteristic of hundreds more, might be cited to remind us of Luther's powerful, and perhaps even dangerous, concentration of the lowly humanity of Jesus. The first is from the early lectures on the Epistle to the Hebrews, 1516-17:

> It is to be noted that he (i.e., the author of the epistle) speaks of the humanity of Christ before he names his deity, and by this approves that rule of knowing God by faith. For his humanity is our holy ladder, by which we ascend to the knowledge of God. . . . Who wishes safely to ascend to the love and knowledge of God, let him leave human and metaphysical rules for knowing the deity, and let him first exercise himself in the humanity of Christ. For it is the most impious of all temerities when God himself has humbled himself in order that he might be knowable, that a man should seek to climb up some other way, through his own ingenious devices (Weimar edition, 57.99.1).

The second is from the lectures on Galatians, delivered in 1531:

> But true Christian divinity (as I give you often warning) setteth not God forth unto us in his majesty, as Moses and other doctrines do. It commandeth us not to search out the nature of God: but to know his will set out to us in Christ, whom he would have to take

our flesh upon him, to be born and to die for our sins.
... Wherefore ... there is nothing more dangerous than
to wander with curious speculations in heaven, and
there to search out God in his incomprehensible power,
wisdom and majesty, how he created the world, and
how he governeth it. ... Therefore begin thou there
where Christ began, namely, in the womb of the Vir-
gin, in the manger, and at his mother's breasts. ... For
to this end he came down, was born, was conversant
among men, suffered, was crucified and died, that by
all means he might set forth himself plainly before our
eyes, and fasten the eyes of our hearts upon himself,
that he thereby might keep us from climbing up into
heaven, and from the curious searching of the divine
majesty. ... Then know thou that there is no other
God besides this man Christ Jesus. ... I know by experience what I say." [9]

In our day, Karl Barth, in the first part of his treatment
of the doctrine of reconciliation, insists over and over
that we must allow Jesus' lowliness and humiliation to
determine what we mean by God. Here are some of his
comments:

How the freedom of God is constituted, in what character He is the Creator and Lord of all things, distinct
from and superior to them, in short, what is to be
understood by 'Godhead,' is something which—watch-
ful against all imported ideas, ready to correct them
and perhaps to let them be reversed and renewed in the

---

[9] From Philip S. Watson's revision of the 1575 English translation
(London: James Clarke & Co., 1953), pp. 43-4.

most astonishing way—we must always learn from Jesus Christ (p. 129).

God shows Himself to be the great and true God in the fact that He can and will let His grace bear this cost, that He is capable and willing and ready for this condescension, this act of extravagance, this far journey (p. 159).

The meaning of His deity—the only true deity in the New Testament sense—cannot be gathered from any notion of supreme, absolute, non-worldly being. It can be learned only from what took place in Christ (p. 177).

Has He really made Himself worldly for the world's sake or not? (p. 196).

God chooses condescension. He chooses humiliation, lowliness and obedience (p. 199).

... in giving Himself up to this alien life in His Son God did not evade the cause of man's fall and destruction, but exposed Himself to and withstood the temptation which man suffers and in which he becomes a sinner and the enemy of God (p. 215).[10]

To speak about God and to know him means, therefore, to shape everything that we say and pray into the pattern of Jesus the humiliated Lord. Can we do this in a pure way? Can we do it so perfectly that all the prob-

---

[10] The page references are to *Church Dogmatics*, Vol. IV, Part 1. It should be pointed out that this note is sounded in the first part of Barth's three-part study of the person and work of Christ. He would doubtless consider the position being suggested here woefully incomplete without the parallel emphasis on the exaltation of man to God alongside the condescension of God to man. The weakness of my position that I indicate just below is not weakness in Barth.

lems of "belief in the time of the death of God" magically disappear? Is there, for the man in Jesus the Lord, no sense of God's withdrawal and hounding presence, no waiting for God? I cannot believe that a decision for Jesus as Lord will so simply make irrelevant the situation that we described a chapter ago. The God of the time of the death of God and the God coming in Jesus the Lord are somehow both with us, and as yet no conceptual way has offered itself that will permit us to assign each an appropriate place. A decision for Jesus as Lord is the way we face our difficulties, the way we turn the corner, the way we put off the threat of unbelief in, or rebellion against, that other kind of divinity. Perhaps some new formulation of the doctrine of the Trinity would be a way to fit the two themes together. But now they are both present; each striking, correcting, and violating the other.

One thing is true. We have chosen to live with the dangers of the impotence or weakness of God rather than with the dangers of his power, for we believe that this was God's choice in the crucifixion. We have gained something, and we have lost something. We have gained the power to say: "because of Jesus the Lord, God is always emptying himself to meet us where we are. In joy and in despair, he will never let us go." But if we have one kind of confidence along these lines, we have deprived ourselves of another kind, that kind which can say: "God's rule cannot be violated, his purposes for his creation are sure, his power stands sure over all earthly powers." We have chosen to stand with his lowly presence, but we have so defined power as weakness, that our life in that presence has lost much of the protection and serenity other Christians have known.

For example, what becomes, along these lines, of the classical Christian refusal to speak of the suffering of God? Patristic orthodoxy, for a number of reasons, always felt that to ascribe suffering directly to God made him a victim of men's evil and deprived him of his role as victor. If the cross means God's participation in suffering, surely the resurrection points to God's victory over suffering. If we ascribe suffering to God, can we ever say that he gives man victory over suffering? If he is a victim in this way of what man can do to him, can he really be said to be God?

The approach taken here means that we have far less uneasiness in ascribing suffering to God than our theological forefathers did. We have taken Jesus' suffering as the key to his Lordship, and if Jesus is ever to be said to confront us with God, the suffering of God must be affirmed, and we will have to correct the distortions this may bring in other ways. In Bonhoeffer's prison poem "Christians and Unbelievers," suffering is ascribed to God, and God's victory over it is not a victory of power but a victory of forgiveness.

Men go to God when they are sore bestead,
Pray to him for succour, for his peace, for bread,
For mercy for them sick, sinning or dead:
All men do so, Christian and unbelieving.

Men go to God when he is sore bestead,
Find him poor and scorned, without shelter or bread,
Whelmed under weight of the wicked, the weak, the dead:
Christians stand by God in his hour of grieving.

God goeth to every man when sore bestead,
Feedeth body and spirit with his bread,
For Christians, heathens alike he hangeth dead:
And both alike forgiving.[11]

The early church was obliged to distinguish the trustworthy God of the Christians from the capricious gods
of popular Graeco-Roman religion. Thus God was called
impassible; unable to participate in *passio*, which sometimes means human feelings, sometimes is very close to
sin itself. In any case, it came to mean that God in himself could not suffer. Impassibility was an indispensable
part of the early doctrine of God, especially when mod-
alism needed to be repudiated. But this god had to be
related somehow to the world of suffering and sin. So
the solution called on the orthodox distinction between
the first two persons of the Trinity: God the Father is
free from suffering, God the Son suffers in the death of
Jesus. However satisfactory this may have been in Ter-
tullian's time, it is not necessarily binding on us. I suspect that a solution along eschatological lines might be
more useful than the trinitarian one. In this world that
we know, we affirm the suffering of God in Jesus the
Lord. Jesus' lordship is now a lordship from the cross.[12]

---

11 *Letters and Papers from Prison*, pp. 167-68.
12 As in Pascal's "Jesus will be in agony until the end of the world."

In the world to come, the suffering lordship will be at an end, God's suffering will cease, and we will come to know him as victor. Perhaps this is something like the distinction hinted at by Paul, in 1 Cor. 15:24-28, between Christ's temporary lordship and God's final rule.

Jesus and the forgiveness of God. To take Jesus as the humiliated Lord, the one who brings us the suffering God, not only clarifies our thinking about the knowledge of God; it provides as well a clue to our understanding of forgiveness. Dr. Tillich and Dr. Bultmann have said a good deal about forgiveness, but it is fairly clear that neither of them needs to depend very much on the man Jesus or on the form of his earthly lordship for their understanding of it. This unwillingness to relate Jesus to the doctrine of forgiveness of sins may be taken as unfortunate, leading to some real inadequacies in their formulations.

Dr. Bultmann represents a tradition of New Testament criticism that does not believe we find in the gospel accounts much trustworthy historical material, and so he is not inclined to use this material in his interpretation of forgiveness. Jesus may be said to "encounter" man. But how? Primarily as the bearer of a message about a new age coming into the midst of man, and as bearer of God's action in bringing the new age to pass. When Jesus is preached, Bultmann says, God is truly met. When he is thus met, man may believe, and thus participate in a new kind of existence, an eschatological existence, as he calls it. Forgiveness is a quality of this new kind of existence, and it means for Bultmann libera-

tion from man's self-bondage, freedom, and the power
to face an open future without fear. Forgiveness does
not lead to action as such, but to a certain posture, or
way of standing before the future. The fact of Jesus is
essential. But details about him, his life, his message, or
his fate, are not as such significant. He brings us God's
act, and therefore Bultmann claims he can accept the
orthodox formulation of Jesus' divinity.[13]

We find a similar approach in Dr. Tillich's writing. In
one sense, Tillich needs to make little use of Jesus in his
understanding of forgiveness of sins. His famous refor-
mulation of justification by faith in the sermon "You
Are Accepted" invites us to see forgiveness as our acceptance of the fact that we are accepted by God, just
as we are, in our sin and doubt. It would not seem from
this that Tillich would need to bring Jesus into his por-
trayal of forgiveness at all. And yet at another point he
seems to imply that the center of the Christian faith is
found in the relationship between the Christian and
Jesus:

> Forget all Christian doctrines; forget your own cer-
> tainties and your own doubts, when you hear the call
> of Jesus. Forget all Christian morals, your achieve-
> ments and your failures, when you come to Him.
> Nothing is demanded of you—no idea of God, and no

---

13 Bultmann's acceptance of the orthodox Christology, in the form
it takes in the World Council of Churches' confession of Jesus Christ
as God and Savior, can be studied in *Essays* (London: SCM Press),
pp. 273-90. His acceptance of this confession is so much like a rejection that his exact relation to classical Christology remains highly
problematic.

goodness in yourselves, not your being religious, not your being Christian, not your being wise, and not your being moral. But what is demanded is only your being open and willing to accept what is given to you, the New Being, the being of love and justice and truth, as it is manifest in Him Whose yoke is easy and Whose burden is light.[14]

But this Jesus is not one about whom anything specific needs to be stated except that he issues a call and that he is the New Being in whom man may participate. The precise form of Jesus' lordship, the form of suffering, is not needed, either here or in a definition of forgiveness as acceptance.[15]

For both men, thus, forgiveness is a central part of the Christian message, but neither of them needs to draw on Jesus the Lord, save as a rather abstract event, act, or possibility of existence. His lowliness, his humiliation, his way of being with men are not seen as significant factors, and can thus play no part in a doctrine of forgiveness.

Dietrich Bonhoeffer describes the Christian's relation to Jesus in quite different terms. This relationship, and the forgiveness that is part of it, is not merely an encoun-

---

[14] *The Shaking of the Foundations*, p. 102.

[15] One of the most illuminating biblical accounts of forgiveness is certainly the story of Jesus and the adulterous woman (John 7:53 to 8:11). Here there is something like the Tillichian "acceptance" ("neither do I condemn you"), but there is also a very "directive" word of judgment ("go, and do not sin again"). Biblical material such as this belongs in any good doctrine of forgiveness, and it is unfortunate when theological or critical assumptions rule it out of court. For it is precisely when we look at Jesus moving among men that a definition of forgiveness as acceptance seems most inadequate.

ter, not merely a call to participation in a new order of reality. It involves careful attention to the precise form of Jesus' life. It is, for Bonhoeffer, discipleship. Just because he sees the close relation of forgiveness and discipleship, he can point out something that we did not notice in the positions of Dr. Bultmann or Dr. Tillich. Being forgiven through Christ is not only God doing something for us, it is the beginning of a way in which we do something to others. Forgiveness involves both our forgiveness and the beginning of the forgiven life among men.

> To be conformed to the image of Christ is not an ideal to be striven after. It is not as though we had to imitate him as well as we could. We cannot transform ourselves into his image, it is rather the form of Christ which seeks to be formed in us.[16]

The earthly image of Christ is the image of the crucified one. Forgiveness is not merely a declaration of independence or a proclaimed word or encounter; it is a bending down to us of God defined by Jesus' work and words. It therefore offers us a precise way in which the forgiven life may be lived. It is more than a posture before the future, more than participation in the New Being. It is a particular way of moving in the world, and this way is given to us as we watch Jesus himself among the men of the world. Thus Jesus the Lord is our way

---

16 *The Cost of Discipleship* (revised and unabridged edition; London: SCM Press, 1959), p. 272. Published in the U. S. by Macmillan Co. (N. Y.).

both to God's forgiveness and to the human forgiveness demanded of the forgiven man. "Discipleship" which dares to use the whole New Testament story in its understanding of forgiveness is thus a more fruitful term than the rather barren "encounter" which, while it may describe how we are freed from ourselves, does not have anything to say about how we are freed for our neighbor.

This leads us to the final question from the beginning of the chapter, and to the final concern of the chapter as a whole. What is the relation between *Jesus and the will of God?* How can the understanding of the lordship of Jesus that we have adopted here help us in our ethical thinking? What is the relation between our Christology and our ethics?

Two preliminary remarks are in order. First, it should be noted that Christology can help us take a stand in the argument in ethical circles today over the legitimacy of moral principles. Does reliance on these advance, or does it weaken, Christian ethical thinking? One group here would say that we are always bound to do God's will, but principles do not help, and each situation must be studied afresh before one comes to a decision as to what God's will in it may be. Others would insist, in various ways, that we can avoid the dreaded foes—moralism and legalism—without going this far, and that there are ways of giving shape to what we mean by God's will apart from the specific context of a decision. I suspect that the latter position has the truth with it, and I think that the way we fill out the content of God's will apart from the situation is to attend to the nature of Jesus' lordship. If we have, in Jesus the Lord, a picture of God coming into the world of men and of decisions in a particular way; if that way can be defined, partly by an inspection of Jesus' life among men, partly by a reflection on his death, as a way of lowliness and suffering—then there are surely precise clues to the meaning of God's will that cannot be dismissed as legalistic precept or moral advice. If we define what we mean by love as what God was doing among men in Jesus the Lord, we have some lines to guide us as we seek to move among men obedient to that Lord. In this sense God's will can be known prior to the particular structures of ethical decision.

A second remark. We have already noted that *kyrios*-Lord in Hellenistic thought referred to a figure to whom absolute loyalty and obedience are owed. When the Christian Church moved into the Hellenistic world with its proclamation that Jesus is the Lord, it meant that Jesus is the way by which the Christian man orders his loyalties. Many earthly loyalties are possible and necessary; even "mammon" or property is necessary, as Jesus himself assumes in Matt. 6:18 ff. It is not that one cannot have many loyalties along with Jesus the Lord. It is that man cannot serve any Lord but Jesus; there is no absolute loyalty permitted other than to God as known in Jesus the Lord. Jesus the Lord is thus not only the content of the will of God; he is the means of ordering all the competing wills that claim our attention. Jesus is thus the only Lord, the only absolute loyalty, but many relative allegiances and commitments are possible under this fundamental one.

LORDSHIP OVER THE WORLD

I think we will move even closer to the center of the relation of Christology and ethics, however, if we reformulate the problem in a slightly different way. Today the nature of Jesus' relation to the world of men is being put, quite properly, in these terms: If Jesus is in fact the Lord, in what sense can he be said to be Lord of the world? What does it mean, what kind of Christology and ethic are implied by the affirmation, now almost a theological cliché, that Jesus is Lord over the world?

There are many who say that this lordship is first of all located in the church, and identified and given its meaning by the internal life of the Christian community.

> Christ is at the same time Lord of this little community which represents his body on earth, and from that very center Sovereign over all the world. We grasp this when we consider that his Lordship is already experienced every time the little community celebrates the Lord's Supper. Thus the Church appears in reality as *the center of Christ's Lordship over the whole world.*[17]

There are a number of senses in which this may be said to be true, but we are surely correct if we confess to some uneasiness with theological statements like this that elevate ecclesiastical existence to such a normative role.

---

[17] From *Christology of the New Testament,* by Oscar Cullmann. © SCM Press, Ltd., 1959. Published in U. S. by the Westminster Press. By permission. Pp. 212-13.

I am not at all sure that Protestants ought to rest too easily with statements that suggest, as Cullmann's does, that the Christian man is most truly himself when he is a man in the church. Catholicism can be so understood; here man is man-in-the-church, and all other relationships are problematic. For Protestantism it can be claimed that man is always man-in-the-world, and all relationships other than this are the problematic ones.

If there is anything to the suggestion of Bonhoeffer that man is moving towards a time of doing without religion at all,[18] we have a further reason to be dissatisfied with the ecclesiastical-sacramental view of the lordship of Christ. Indeed, in his posthumously published *Ethics*, Bonhoeffer tried to reformulate the idea of lordship over the world so that it might meet this kind of objection. "There are not two realities," he wrote, "but only one reality, and that is the reality of God, which has become manifest in Christ in the reality of the world.... The whole reality of the world is already drawn in into Christ and bound together in Him."[19] It is in the world, not the church, where Christ's lordship is known, so Bonhoeffer can go on to say that what is distinctively Christian is found only in the secular, "the 'supernatural' only in the natural, the holy only in the profane, and the revelational only in the rational."[20] Bonhoeffer acknowledged that this position meant a decisive repudiation of Luther's idea of the devil as the prince and ruler of this

---

[18] *Letters and Papers from Prison*, pp. 122-26.
[19] *Ethics*, pp. 63, 64.
[20] *Ibid.*, p. 65.

world. "The world is not divided between Christ and the devil, but whether it recognizes it or not, it is solely and entirely the world of Christ." [21]

There is some evidence, however, that Bonhoeffer later came to repudiate his repudiation of Luther, and moved away from the radically realized view of eschatology that these passages suggest. But he never moved away from what might be called the anti-ecclesiastical approach to Christ's lordship, and there is a real sense in which the whole of Bonhoeffer's later work can be read as the beginning of a systematic attempt to face the theological task by doing without a special doctrine of the church.[22] There is, instead, the worldliness of God and the refusal to work with a rigid church-world distinction. Thus, Bonhoeffer can state that the church has nothing to do, in the first instance, "with the so-called religious functions of man, but with the whole man in his existence in the world with all its implications." [23] This means that a very important implication of the lordship of Christ over the world is the demand it contains for a specific theological appreciation of the secular. But what would this mean, and how would it be worked out?

To say that Jesus is Lord is to say that humiliation,

---

[21] *Ibid.*, p. 70.

[22] This is not an interpretation of Bonhoeffer, needless to say, that would commend itself to ecumenical theologians in our day, and it should be noted that several of the writers in the volumes of papers on Bonhoeffer, *Die Mündige Welt* (Munich: Kaiser Verlag), propose as the clue to Bonhoeffer the doctrine of the church.

[23] *Ethics*, p. 21.

patience, and suffering are the ways God has dealt with
man in the world, and thus are also the ways the Christian man is to deal with the world. This means that the
Christian cannot say to the world "we want you to be
like us," but rather "we want you to be yourself." Christianity and church are not everything, and the world has
its own rights apart from, even in rebellion against, Christianity. Furthermore, this willingness to let the world be
the world means that Christianity will not always be
busily interpreting the problems of the world as ones it
is peculiarly fitted to meet.[24] Professor Gregor Smith has
remarked that the perhaps overpraised ecumenical movement may not break out of its impasse until it learns, in
its theology, to take more seriously the needs of the secular world. This requires, he says,

> a temper and a quality of mind which will allow the
> world to be itself and in loving humility to elicit from
> the world's achievements and from its failures the possibilities which might lead it further.... The Church
> cannot stand over the world with a whip; nor can it get
> behind it with a load of dynamite.[25]

---

[24] In our day this pseudo-affection for the secular is a special temptation to the Christian apologist. Every time an artist or a dramatist
suggests something of the brokenness of life, we attempt to adopt him
immediately as part of the preparation for the Gospel. Lionel Trilling
wrote recently: "Can anything be more depressing than the round-eyed seriousness with which the more-or-less educated American
middle class takes the notions about life of the modern American
dramatist?" *The Mid-Century*, No. 3 (September, 1959).

[25] *The New Man* (London: SCM Press, 1956), p. 68. Published in
the U. S. by Harper & Bros. (N. Y.).

As the Lord identified himself with men without reserve, as he stood beside men offering for their free and un-coerced choice a particular way, and as he did this for their own sakes and not for the success of his movement or career—so the Christian must do in the secular world. A recovery of this line of thinking today can do much to clarify our thinking on Christian ethics, and can per-haps give the church a way out of its curious dilemma of being so secularized in the bad sense that it cannot speak to the secular world in any true sense.

We have come to this: the world is God's; Jesus is Lord of the world; this lordship is received by the Chris-tian as he stands and works in the world; the form of his action is the form of Jesus' lordship. We can begin to explore this problem of a theology of the secular based on the lordship of Jesus by calling attention to an inter-esting tension in Bonhoeffer's later thought. It can be seen by setting down two passages. The first is the one already cited from the *Ethics*.

> There are not two realities, but only one reality, and that is the reality of God which has become manifest in Christ in the reality of the world.... The whole reality of the world is already drawn in into Christ and bound together in Him.... The world is not di-vided between Christ and the devil, but, whether it recognizes it or not, it is solely and entirely the world of Christ.[26]

---

[26] *Ethics*, pp. 63, 64, 70.

The second is one of the final things he wrote, and it
seems to mark a significant shift from the earlier position
in the *Ethics*.

> Man is challenged to participate in the sufferings of
> God at the hands of a godless world. He must there-
> fore plunge himself into the life of a godless world,
> without attempting to gloss over its ungodliness with
> a veneer of religion or trying to transfigure it. He
> must live a "worldly" life and so participate in the
> suffering of God.... To be a Christian does not mean
> to be religious in a particular way, to cultivate some
> particular form of asceticism (as a sinner, a penitent
> or a saint), but to be a man. It is not some religious act
> which makes a Christian what he is, but participation
> in the suffering of God in the life of the world.[27]

In a basic sense, these two passages agree. Man's place
is to stand with God, in Jesus, in the midst of the world.
There is no *real* distinction between church and world,
between religion and the *saeculum*. But in another sense,
the second passage seems to be a correction, if not a kind
of repudiation, of the first. In the first, the world is
wholly Christ's, already drawn in into him; in the sec-

---

[27] *Letters and Papers from Prison*, p. 166. (For an earlier formulation of this, see the revised edition of *The Cost of Discipleship*, p. 42.)
This was written just two days before the July 20, 1944, plot against
Hitler's life, the failure of which assured Bonhoeffer of the inevi-
tability of his own execution. A letter of July 21, written after he had
heard of the failure, returned to the same theme. The idea of the
suffering of God is also touched on in the prison poem "Christians
and Unbelievers," quoted above on pp. 96-7 and found in the *Letters
and Papers from Prison* on pp. 167-68.

ond, the world is godless. In the first, we find an uncompromising rejection of any dualistic view of the world; in the second, we find religion (and thus perhaps including the "religious" solution he had come to in *Ethics?*) accused of covering up the world's godlessness.

The disagreement is not over the necessary worldliness of Christian man. Both passages affirm that man's place is in the world. But we do find two differing interpretations of the meaning and form of Jesus' lordship itself. In the passage from *Ethics*, "lordship" seems to mean the completed redemptive work of God, the summing up in Jesus of all things, in heaven and on earth. It reflects, we might say, a realized view of eschatology and salvation. The second passage defines lordship as God's suffering identification with the world in Jesus, God's lowliness, Jesus' dereliction and suffering, his being at the mercy of the world.

Precisely here, I am sure, is a great gift of Bonhoeffer to our thought and life today: his understanding of what it means to stand in this world in obedience to Jesus the Lord. His earlier confident rejection of Luther's view of the world as in the hands of the devil now seems partly set aside. Can it be true that the world is one that both belongs to Jesus the Lord, yet is at the same time godless? When he writes, "Now that it has come of age, the world is more godless, and perhaps it is for that very reason nearer to God than ever before," [28] we recall the ambiguity of the word "world" in the New Testament

---

[28] *Ibid.*, p. 167. Compare this statement to the discussion above of the relation of doubt and faith, pp. 60 ff.

itself. "World" is both that which God loved in sending Jesus to his death (John 3:16), and that which crucified him. The New Testament never cleanly resolves this problem: Jesus' death is done by God out of his love for the world, and it is also done by the world's hatred of God (Acts 2:23; 4:27 ff.). If this kind of solution is possible, then in these Bonhoeffer citations there is not a real contradiction, but a development and enrichment of his thought, brought about by the fateful events of the final years of his life.

All this means, I suspect, that the quality of the Christological ethic we derive from our belief in the lordship of Jesus over the world depends on our reading very carefully what can be called the almost unbearable eschatological tension in the presence of which the events of the New Testament are lived. In the synoptic gospels, the world is in the hands of the kingdom of Satan, and Jesus is engaged in a massive attack on the world. Individual victories are achieved when healing is done, when demons are cast out. The kingdom or lordship is present, concealed perhaps, but present, in the healing ministry itself (Luke 11:20 and Matt. 12:28). But the enemy is also present, from the temptations at the start of the ministry to Gethsemane and the cry of dereliction at its close. In Jesus' teaching, the world meant mammon, anxiety, and self-righteousness. He asks us not to flee these, not to proclaim them already conquered, but to destroy them.[29]

---

29 Harnack, *What is Christianity?* p. 84, is excellent at this point.

In Paul, we find a tension between salvation as already achieved, as coming in the present, and as yet to come. His terms are not those of the gospels, but he too knows that in this world there must be a looking forward from a present imperfection to a fulfillment to come (Rom. 8:22, 23). True, we have been saved (Rom. 8:24; 10:10), we are now justified (Rom. 5:1, 9), we have peace and access to God's grace (Rom. 5:1-2). But it is also true that we shall be saved (Rom. 5:9, 10), we rejoice in our hope (Rom. 5:2), and salvation is nearer than before, though not yet wholly here (Rom. 13:11). If this tension in the New Testament between present and future is something we cannot explain away in the material, if it stands as an essential part of the record for us, then our view of the quality of Christ's lordship will be affected. He is King, but incognito in this world. He is the Lord, but he is the Lord who is away, for whom we the servants still in some sense wait. (For an insight into the early church's strong sense of waiting for the Lord, compare Luke 19:11-27 and Matthew 25:14-30 on the parable of the talents.)

If we keep our eschatology straight, we will find ourselves saying both "Jesus is Lord of the world" and "Jesus will be Lord of the world." His present lordship has one form, the form of suffering and service and hiddenness; his lordship to come will have the form of victory and power. Even in the gospel according to John, which of all the gospels most stresses the completed work of God, we read the words of Jesus to the disciples: "In the world you have tribulation; but be of good cheer, I

have overcome the world" (16:33). Not "I have overcome your tribulation" and not "you have overcome the
world," and not even "if you try, you can overcome the
world." But, "I have, and in God's time, because I have,
you shall overcome it too." The resurrection and exaltation of Jesus is the one point in this world where the
manifest lordship has been revealed. In the meantime, in
the time between the resurrection and the end, whatever
that may be, the world still hurts us, it still bears its
demons that need to be exorcised, it still contains mammon, anxiety, and self-righteousness that need to be
fought.

We need to be very clear, therefore, about this distinction between the two forms of Jesus' lordship over
the world. These two forms are different in quality: one
a lordship of humiliation, the other a lordship of victory
and power. And they are different in time; the one is a
lordship for now; the other is a lordship that is to come,
or that we are to come to. Too much of the church's
use of the formula "Christ is Lord of the world" is de-
ficient both in Christology (it does not perceive clearly
enough the form of the suffering lordship) and in eschatology (it forgets the tension between the present and
the future forms of that lordship). We are now the
Lord's, to be sure, and this is our confidence, our peace,
and our warrant for living gladly in this world; but we
shall be the Lord's too, and this explains our loneliness,
our suffering, our experience of the world as threat and
as enemy.

Historic Christianity has had a far more vivid sense of

the tension between this-worldliness and otherworldliness than we have today. We seem to move, much more anxiously than our forefathers did, between the extremes of pietistic otherworldliness and heartiness or crypto-secularism.[30]

Perhaps for many of us the latter is a special temptation, and with this goes a fear of otherworldliness. We fear, perhaps, that it commits us to a belief in the existence of some space beyond the known space of this world, and this we find very hard to believe. The ease with which we have accepted an existentialist redefinition of God as the meaning of *this* life, *this* existence, shows that we are unable to stand as Christians in a life that may, strictly speaking, be meaningless and unintelligible. Otherworldliness, stripped of its geographical problems, would be a real boon.[31]

---

[30] Augustine, in *The City of God* (XXII. 22-24.), places cheek by jowl a detailed analysis of the miseries of the present life which is harrowing to read, and a description of "the blessings with which the Creator has filled this life, obnoxious though it be to the curse." And Calvin, in a section that bears the marks of his profound knowledge of Augustine, has an extremely otherworldly, even antiworldly "meditation on the future life" coming just before a beautiful chapter on "the right use of the present life and its supports," which would have delighted an Erasmus, or even a Shakespeare (*Institutes*, III. 9 and 10).

[31] In a letter dated March 20, 1915, Von Hügel notes the absence in William Temple of the dimension of Christianity as "the awakening souls to, the preparing them for, the holding before them embodiments of, *the other life*, the life beyond the grave. Very certainly the church has also to help in the amelioration of *this life*; but, I submit, always after, and in subordination to, and penetrated by, that metaphysical, ontological, otherworldly sense and life which alone completes and satisfies fully awakened man." From *Selected Letters* (London: J. M. Dent, 1928), p. 220.

If we want to hold to a proper otherworldliness and still take seriously the task of working out a proper Christian understanding of the secular, we must do this with a much more careful understanding of Jesus' lordship over the world than we have yet managed. In what sense is he our Lord; in what sense is he now Lord over the world; and in what sense will he be the Lord? Perhaps we ought to remember the insight of Luther (which we saw Bonhoeffer rebelling against and later returning to) that this world is in the hands of the devil.[32] Robert Frost may have confounded many of his admirers when he said recently, "It is a coarse, brutal world, unendurably coarse and brutal, for anyone who hasn't the least dash of coarseness or brutality in his own nature to enjoy it with." [33] This is a word Luther would have loved. The position adopted here on the lordship of Jesus enables us to receive the pessimism of a Luther, a Freud, or a Frost, but it is for us a pessimism without despair. We have a way of speaking of hope even while agreeing with Silone when he declares that "in the sacred history of man on earth, it is still, alas, Good Friday." [34]

---

[32] Luther's position has recently received a fascinating defense in Norman Brown's brilliant *Life Against Death* (Wesleyan University Press, 1960). The book is primarily a study of Freud, and it notes that Luther's position is confirmed by Freud's pessimistic conviction, which Brown defends, of the universality of neurosis in our culture.

[33] Quoted in a review article in *The New York Times*, Sunday, June 19, 1960.

[34] My agreement with this statement, and my strong emphasis on the cross and on lordship as humiliation, will suggest to many that I have deliberately ignored that portion of the Christian kerygma that speaks of ascension, exaltation, and all that goes with the kingly office.

If this picture of Jesus as Lord has anything to be said for it, there is one further question to ask. What is the quality of the Christian life that can spring from such a vision of God, Jesus, and the world? Even this fragmentary statement of how we are to believe must be followed by some attempt to state how we are to live. This is our final task.

This is quite true; this has been ignored. It is not because I find it false or irrelevant, but because I do not see how one can give this extremely important part of the work of Christ any precise meaning today. It is just that I do not understand it, and I do not really understand those who tell me what it means. One important exception to this is Jesus' resurrection. I do not believe that my position here implies any particular view or non-view of the resurrection. As a matter of fact, I find myself in fairly strenuous opposition to that tradition in contemporary theology which denies the resurrection as an ordinary event on the one hand, while giving it a profound existential meaning on the other. I believe that the resurrection of Jesus can be affirmed as an ordinary event; the empty tomb tradition, at least, seems to me to contain historical material of a high degree of probability. The historical texture to this event is not equivalent to its meaning for faith, but there can be no meaning for faith, I am sure, without this historical texture. In the context of this chapter, I would argue that the resurrection means the making present and available to men of faith the form of Jesus' lordship as a form of humiliation and suffering. He is risen, with the marks of his suffering still upon him.

Chapter Four

CHAPTER 4

The Style of the Christian Life

Sed in hac quaestione Deum videndi, plus mihi videtur valere vivendi modus, quam loquendi. (But on this matter of the vision of God, the style of life seems to me more important than the style of speech.)

— William of Saint-Thierry

In the first chapter, we suggested that one of the marks of an essence of Christianity for our time might be a certain tone or quality to our theological speech—a quality of modesty, waiting, patience. But if there is a proper Christian rhetoric, there is also of course a Christian ethic. I should like to set down some of the marks of a possible ethic for our time by making use of the phrase "style of life." It is, I believe, an important phrase to try to understand.

To say that the Christian faith must lead to a distinctive style of life is, first of all, to say a very obvious thing. It is to say that a man's confession of Jesus as Lord ought never to be tested merely by what he says, but primarily

119

by what it looks like as worked out in his life. Unless the Christian vision, however fragmentary it may be, spills over into the way a man moves and acts in the world, the vision is not really Christian at all, however correct the words may be that describe it.

"Style of life" means something more. It suggests that the Christian faith is lived out, not only in the realm of work, not only in the so-called orders of creation or in the public realm, but in privacy as well. "Style of life" belongs to what can be called personal—as against social —ethics. Protestant ethics since the Reformation has been almost exclusively work-oriented, and it is very difficult to find anything resembling a Protestant doctrine of privacy, leisure, or play. W. B. Yeats has written:

> The intellect of man is forced to choose
> Perfection of the life, or of the work,
> And if it take the second must refuse
> A heavenly mansion, raging in the dark.
> When all that story's finished, what's the news?
> In luck or out the toil has left its mark:
> That old perplexity an empty purse,
> Or the day's vanity, the night's remorse.[1]

It may be arguable whether such a choice is necessary; but if it is, Yeats is right to urge us work-oriented activists to choose perfection of life. The phrase "style of life" helps us point to some of the things such a struggle for perfection might involve.

---

[1] "The Choice," *The Collected Poems of W. B. Yeats* (New York: Macmillan Co., 1958), p. 242.

There is one quite proper and correct way of giving content to the Christian style of life. That is to say that the pattern of the Christian life is the man Jesus: he is true man, man as he ought to be. But I am not at all sure that this correct way is a very helpful way. For the truth of the matter is that we really do not know enough about Jesus as a man before men; this is largely hidden from us. And though "our lives are hid with Christ in God," our lives, insofar as they are Christian, cannot be wholly invisible. We are asked to let our light shine before men. And as greatly as we fear too pious religious or moral display, there is no escape from a demand for concrete visibility of some kind. We have, I fear, allowed Kierkegaard's words about the incognito character of the knight of faith to serve as an excuse for our not pressing toward some kind of visibility. Now we know something of Jesus the man, but it is not enough for the kind of visibility we need. We know him as the lowly one, humiliated, totally at the disposal of the other; he is in this sense Lord. This is central, but in itself it cannot automatically become in us a style of life appropriate for the demands of our time and place and vocation.

Therefore the struggle to define a Christian style of life for our time may have to forego, at least provisionally, the simplicity and correctness of the *imitatio Christi*. What, then, can such a style be? What does it entail? It is something more than the style of speech we have already mentioned. But it is also something less than specific actions. This style is a way of standing before God and the world, a posture—as it has come to be called—

that is prior to, and basic to, any and all actions and decisions. It is, as Silone puts it,

> not a matter of putting new formulas, new gestures, of shirts of a different color into circulation, but rather a matter of a new way of living.... It is a matter of becoming a new man. Perhaps it is sufficient to say that it is a matter of becoming a man, in the real sense of the word.[2]

It is not an answer to the pilgrim's cry "What shall I do?" but an answer to a more difficult and fundamental question, "What shall I be?"

In what way does a style of life deserve a claim to be called Christian? There are no direct lines from the New Testament to the style of life I will be defending, and there are more than a few indirect lines from secular culture contributing to it. I would claim that the vision of the lordship of Jesus, sketched out in the previous chapter, is in some way determinative of this style. But at the same time, a similar style can be both described and lived without this confession of lordship. Even if the style should prove to be imperfectly Christian in definition, I would still insist—not that it need be, but—that it can be chosen by the Christian man with integrity and a good conscience.[3]

---

[2] *Bread and Wine*, p. 291.

[3] Erik Erikson has defined integrity in words that are appropriate: "It is the acceptance of one's one and only life cycle as something that had to be and that, by necessity, permitted no substitutions.... Although aware of the relativity of all the various life styles which have given meaning to human striving, the possessor of integrity is

THE STYLE OF LIFE—A FIRST SKETCH

Some words of Camus will help us.

> "It comes to this," Tarrou said almost casually; "what interests me is learning how to become a saint."
>
> "But you don't believe in God."
>
> "Exactly. Can one be a saint without God?—that's the problem, in fact that's the only problem I'm up against today." [4]

We who are not wholly without God might well define the problem of the style of life as a struggle for sainthood. What does it mean to be a saint in the world, a secular saint? Let us make a beginning by setting down several random guidelines.

1. *A sense of reserve or reticence in our dealings with others.* In the midst of the enthusiastic interest in Bonhoeffer's fragmentary comments on the non-religious interpretation of Christianity, another, and perhaps more interesting, comment of his has largely gone unnoticed. I have borrowed this first guideline directly from him.

---

ready to defend the dignity of his own life style against all physical and economic threats. For he knows that an individual life is the accidental coincidence of but one life cycle with but one segment of history; and that for him all human integrity stands or falls with the one style of integrity of which he partakes." From *Childhood and Society*, p. 232, quoted in the same author's *Young Man Luther*, pp. 260-61.

[4] A. Camus, *The Plague*, pp. 230-31. This figure of the saint without God is found in a number of places in Camus' work. One finds it also in Silone, particularly *Bread and Wine;* and perhaps also in Koestler's *Darkness at Noon*.

Unless we have the courage to fight for a revival of a wholesome reserve between man and man, all human values will be submerged in anarchy. . . . Where self-respect is abandoned, where the feeling for human quality and the power of reserve decay, chaos is at the door. . . . Our duty today . . . is passionately to defend the sense of reserve between man and man. We shall be accused of acting for our own interests, of being anti-social. . . . Socially it implies the cessation of all place-hunting, of the cult of the "star." It requires an open eye both upwards and downwards, especially in the choice of one's closest friends. Culturally it means a return from the newspaper and the radio to the book, from feverish activity to unhurried leisure, from dissipation to recollection, from sensationalism to reflection, from virtuosity to art, from snobbery to modesty, from extravagance to moderation.[5]

This reserve is partly defined by noting its opposites, heartiness and frankness. It suggests that the way to another person—like the way to a true idea or a beautiful object—is a slow and difficult way. It reminds us that mere talk and mere being together do not suffice.

Reserve also means a willingness to leave the other person alone, to let him be himself, apart from us. It means that there is in every man a center in which an "other" does not belong. There must be a genuine "space" between man and man, lest, seeing so clearly the dangers of destroying another by arrogance and hostility, we find

---

[5] *Letters and Papers from Prison*, pp. 22-3.

ourselves destroying him by love, forgiveness, or acceptance. Thus, reserve means respect for the other's right to
solitariness, and a defense both for ourselves and for the
other of the rights of privacy and solitude. Respect
means giving the other a full right to be apart from us,
apart from society, alone.[6] Thus Bonhoeffer is correct
when he notes, in the above passage, that the defender of
reserve may find himself accused of being antisocial. In
many ordinary areas of life this ability to grant respect
to the other comes into play: the way we choose and
entertain our friends, the way we relax and play, the kind
of house we plan and build. This reserve is, I believe, a
large element in what we mean by "love" of the neighbor. It suggests a closeness and a distance between one
and another, both of which surely an authentic human
love must have.

2. *A combination of tolerance and anger.* At the close
of his sprightly essay, "Christianity, Liberalism, and Liberality," Alec Vidler defines the kind of Christian man
he would like to see emerge in contemporary culture:
"the man who is tolerant, not because he regards all opin-
ions as doubtful, but because he knows that God alone
is true,—the man who is ready to learn from all men, not
because he has no creed of his own, but because his creed
assures him that God is teaching and chastening all men,
—the man who has plumbed the meaning for the human
intellect of the great New Testament word about having

---

[6] Norman Brown, in *Life Against Death*, speaks of sociability as
a sickness, of "the morbidity of human sociability" (p. 105).

nothing and yet possessing all things,—the man who can at once rigorously doubt and sincerely believe . . ." [7]

Tolerance is one of the ways we are called to stand in the presence of what disturbs, threatens, or displeases us. But at the other end of the spectrum lies anger, and this is equally legitimate and necessary. George Orwell concludes his essay on Dickens with this defense of anger:

> He is laughing, with a touch of anger in his laughter, but no triumph, no malignity. It is the face of a man who is always fighting against something, but who fights in the open and is not frightened, the face of a man who is *generously angry*—in other words, of a nineteenth-century liberal, a free intelligence, a type hated with equal hatred by all the smelly little orthodoxies which are now contending for our souls. [8]

What Orwell means by generous anger is neatly indicated by his final lines about smelly orthodoxies, among which he certainly intends to include the Christian version.

If reserve is that part of a Christian style of life that deals in general with our relation to another person, the tolerance-anger polarity is the part that deals with other persons, groups, and ideas that are in opposition to us. This polarity can be put in Christian language in two

---

[7] *Essays in Liberality* (London: SCM Press, 1957), p. 28.
[8] From the essay on Charles Dickens from *Such, Such Were the Joys,* by George Orwell. Copyright 1945, 1952, 1953, by Sonia Brownell Orwell. Reprinted by permission of Harcourt, Brace & World, Inc.

quite different ways. We know both tolerance and anger, because God shows both to us: his toleration of us is extreme—it leads even to forgiveness; but his anger with us is real, for we easily turn our backs on him and make a mockery of both his name and his demands. We can be trusted to tolerate, to accept, and to forgive, because he has shown these to us. We can also be trusted to be angry without destroying the object of our anger, because we have been refined by his anger and wrath. Or, more simply, the career of Jesus exemplifies both tolerance and anger: to the broken, rejected, and lost, there is his openness and love; to the proud and secure, there is his anger and scorn.

But no Christianization of the tolerance-anger polarity gives us a rule of thumb for balancing the two in any concrete decision. At times, we may need to use each in its pure form; more often, perhaps, our tolerance must have a little anger embedded in it to save us from empty-headed indifference, and our anger must have a concealed tolerance to keep us from absolutism or tyranny. Tolerance, we must remember, is fairly easy for the protected and the strong, for those who are not the victims of intolerance, whereas anger is easy and legitimate for the weak, the unprotected, for those who have no one to defend them. A Christian style of life should possess both weapons, for the Christian knows that there is never a moment when his decisions are not worked out in the midst of conflicting and competing wills to his own.

3. "*Renounce . . . every hope or wish for more than toleration.*" Baron von Hügel often referred to a saying

of Duchesne that had meant a great deal to him in his
own life:

> Work away in utter sincerity and open-mindedness;
> lead as deep and devoted a spiritual life as you can;
> renounce, from the first and every day, every hope or
> wish for more than toleration; and then, with those
> three activities and dispositions, trust and wait, with
> indomitable patience and humility, to be tolerated and
> excused.[9]

Many points in this call for comment. There is the remark about the spiritual life, a concern that so many
have learned from von Hügel. I am not sure just what
can be said about the role of private prayer in the style
of life I am trying to sketch. I would like to see it included, yet I am deeply aware of my inability to say
enough about it from the inside. One can perhaps become a Christian without prayer, but surely one cannot
stay Christian without it. So little is said today about
private prayer in our kind of culture that makes real
sense, and I do not wish to add to the empty invitations
to pray that one finds on every hand.

> Only the works of praying men have remained truly
> alive: Schuetz, Bach, Haydn and Mozart prayed, so
> did Giotto and Angelico, Donatello, Corneille, Racine,
> Pascal and Newton. The humbugs who do not pray
> usually disappear in a few years' time, to be replaced
> by other humbugs. And those who pray are torn in

---

[9] *Selected Letters*, p. 88.

pieces by the non-praying populace like Orpheus by the Maenades, but even then they do not cease their music.[10]

I read this and my first reaction is one of rebellion: what a foolish and self-righteous oversimplification! And yet, perhaps I am trying to cover my own ineptness in prayer by this reaction. Perhaps there is more sense in this exaggeration than I want to see. That those who try to pray are torn to pieces is true enough; this much we all know. Yet they are torn not only by the non-praying ones, but also by themselves. All we know is that somehow our style of life must make room, in our world of noise and movement, for the silence, the waiting, the withdrawal of the life of prayer. Perhaps the secular saint today can never know the ecstasy of the older and wiser saints of the church; perhaps he can know only the experience of being torn apart in the midst of his failure to pray.

There is another point we can be clear about in the saying von Hügel cites. A Christian style of life will include a patient and humble attention to one's daily work, and a firm decision to ask nothing of the world except toleration, indifference, being allowed to get on. This may sound very anti-heroic, and even bourgeois, to some. I would rather say that the only kind of heroism that should interest us is a kind that nobody notices. To ask from the world nothing but toleration is to refuse to be bound by the conformity-non-conformity antith-

[10] Von Balthasar, *op. cit.*, p. 56.

esis that so many are pushing at us these days. If one had to choose between the two, and we don't, most of us would doubtless choose a little bit of the first and a good deal of the second. But to defend the kind of indifference to the world that asking only for toleration implies really undercuts the distinction between conformity and non-conformity. In many ways, of course, the world's needs and our perception of them will set us our tasks; and no one would defend indifference in this wider sense. But indifference in a narrower sense means this: once we have set about our work, we need not spend our time taking bearings from our culture in order to test what we do. Both the free Christian and the free secularist will have bearings to take and a direction to work out; but each will know that the world's estimate of him is the least appropriate source for such guidance. One of the real reasons today for the increasing communication between the Christian and the secularist at certain important levels is the perception that they are common allies in this particular struggle. The free Christian is more at home with the free secularist than with the conventional other-directed Christian for just this reason. As soon as the Christian gets too tired to fight for this precious freedom from the world, the secularism that continues the fight may well prove to be a more attractive option.

4. *A recovery of goodness.* Commenting on Brutus, Professor Goddard wrote that "a man should have no more acquaintance with his virtue than a woman with

her beauty." [11] This aphoristic truth enshrines the age-long suspicion of Western man, and particularly of Christian man, that the worst evil is that of a goodness that calls attention to itself. In our time, it is interesting and a little odd to note, our best theology has written most wisely about the sins following upon goodness, while the daily papers have been busy describing the evils done by evil men to good men. Theology has dissected the subtle temptations of self-righteousness: arrogant, intransigeant, and moralistic goodness. And while we pulled apart the Pharisee, the tyrant has remained to teach us what real evil can be. Perhaps it was his own experience of tyranny that led Bonhoeffer to write:

> It was the experience of other times that the wicked found their way to Christ while the good remained remote from Him. The experience of our own time is that it is the good who find their way back to Christ and that the wicked obstinately remain aloof from Him. Other times could preach that a man must first become a sinner, like the publican and the harlot, before he could know and find Christ, but we in our time must say rather that before a man can know and find Christ he must first become righteous like those who strive and suffer for the sake of justice, truth and humanity.[12]

A Christian style of life must include an unashamed defense of goodness. Our secular saint will be a good man.

---

[11] Harold C. Goddard, *The Meaning of Shakespeare* (Chicago: University of Chicago Press, 1951), p. 311.

[12] *Ethics,* p. 182.

And if we dare not say exactly what this means, we can set down a few suggestions, too modest for some, but valuable for others, just because of their obviousness. Such goodness might well involve: gentleness, sensitivity to the needs and claims of others; willingness to be counted with the underdog in our society; opposition to all coercion, pompousness, injustice, restriction of legitimate freedom; refusal to call attention to one's own goodness, such as it is. There are, of course, many good reasons why such lists of virtues by themselves cannot lead to goodness, and may even frustrate, rather than help, the struggle for goodness. Psychiatry knows some of these reasons, theology knows others. But, however true it is that one cannot become good by willing to be good, this can never mean that a man's moral character is wholly fortuitous and independent of his particular acts of discipline, will, or prayer.

Goodness is, of course, not enough. The man of the world will remind us that there are many places in the world's work where goodness is impossible, where too much goodness will destroy the good man, and where insistence on the good will rule out the possible. And the Christian will still have to point out the temptations of goodness which come mainly when it becomes conscious of itself, noting that forgiveness is always a profounder gift. All of this is true. We can grant that the human personality may have a very low receptivity to injunctions from its own will, and still hold on to our defense of the good man. The secular saint, the man struggling for a Christian style of life, while always open for the possibility of a radical and heroic act of faith in the world, will still not reject the demands for a humbler goodness that his non-heroic hours require.

AN HISTORICAL ASIDE

Before we go more carefully into a description of a Christian style of life for our time, we might pause and look at our Protestant tradition for some clues as to how we came to where we are. The secular saint I am defending is no new figure; he is very much a product of the Protestant Reformation and some later interpretations of it.

We have already called attention to a basic difference between Luther and Calvin in their understanding of God and his relation to the finite world. There is also a difference in how each saw man's relation to the world. Luther said that the world can contain God, but that the world cannot be significantly shaped by God's men. Since God came fully into the finite world in Christ in lowliness and suffering, man obeys this God in the world by the same lowliness and suffering. Calvin, on the other hand, insisted that while the world cannot fully contain God, it nevertheless can be significantly shaped by God's men. Since God has not been fully received by the finite in Christ, the Christian man is bound to enter the world, to shape it and to form there the holy community to God's glory.

There are striking differences between these two views, but there is first to be noted a basic similarity. The place of the Christian is in the world, not out of it. Both the reformers turned consciously away from traditional ascetism towards what Max Weber termed *innerweltliche askese:* inner-worldly; this-worldly; or perhaps best, secular asceticism. The cardinal importance to both Luther and Calvin of the doctrine of vocation, or the calling, should make their basic agreement clear. But, once this agreement has been observed, the two reformers looked at the meaning of secular asceticism in somewhat different ways. Max Weber saw part of this difference,[13] pointing out that the intense worldly activity stimulated by Calvinism was largely a means by which the Protestant man gained confidence about his own election. While Weber did observe that Luther's doctrine of vocation implied a less active concern to transform the world, he did not uncover the real tension between the two reformers.

R. H. Tawney followed up Weber's lead in trying to locate the historical connection between Calvinism and capitalism, and noted that for Calvin "good works are not a way of attaining salvation, but they are indispensable as a proof that salvation has been attained." This meant, Tawney noted, that in the Calvinist form of secular asceticism God's glory is at least partly to be sought in "the sanctification of the world by strife and labor." [14]

Ernst Troeltsch was the one who saw very clearly the

---

[13] See *The Protestant Ethic and the Spirit of Capitalism* (London: Allen and Unwin, Ltd., 1936), Chapter IV.

[14] *Religion and the Rise of Capitalism* (New York: Harcourt Brace & Co., 1926), p. 109.

differences between Luther and Calvin in this sphere of man's relation to the world.[15] Asceticism, he noted, always has two elements: depreciation of the world and systematic discipline of the senses. When Protestant asceticism became worldly, Luther and Calvin took different directions, Luther emphasizing depreciation of the world (that is, of man's power to shape the world), Calvin emphasizing the discipline of the senses. For Luther, there is no plan or law by which man may master the world; discipline in the world is left to the conscience of the individual. In the Lutheran tradition, there is some reluctance to take part, as a Christian, in the work of the world, and this can lead to a kind of endurance, a submission, a rejoicing in the sufferings which the world can bring. It is better to suffer evil than to do good, Luther once declared. This position is combined, in Luther, with a joyous and grateful acceptance of the good things of life as all coming from God. Calvin and Calvinism are more active and aggressive in relation to the world; the Calvinist man wishes to shape the world into a more suitable instrument for the glory of God, to create a Christian commonwealth. The church is thus the disciplined and disciplinary community; the Christian is sober, serious, earnest; nothing in the world is irrelevant to God's purpose. Troeltsch summarized the difference between the two reformers in this way.

---

[15] *The Social Teaching of the Christian Churches,* English translation by Olive Wyon (New York: Macmillan Co., 1931), Vol. II, pp. 605 ff.

Lutheranism endures the world in suffering, pain, and martyrdom, Calvinism masters it for the honour of God by untiring work, for the sake of the self-discipline which work supplies, and the well being of the Christian community which may be attained by means of it.[16]

The point of this historical sketch is to suggest that, in many ways today, the time of the dominance of the Calvinist image is at an end. William H. Whyte, in *The Organization Man*,[17] has written of the decline of the Protestant ethic. If he means by this (which he may not) the Calvinist idea of man's relation to the world, he is certainly correct. The sit-in movement in the South seems to imply a non-Calvinist idea of how the world is shaped; it is more like an extremely subtle mixture of the Lutheran and Calvinist ways, a use of suffering as a means of exercising power. This is perhaps the reason this movement has both bewildered many Christian ethical realists and excited so many young people. Or again: the bourgeois conformist and the beat, apparently as unlike each other as grey flannel is unlike blue jeans, are

---

[16] *Protestantism and Progress*, the English translation, 1912; this citation taken from pp. 84-5 of the reprint by Beacon Press (Boston, 1958). The section from pp. 80-5 is relevant to this point. We can see why, in the sixteenth century, when men came to have the experience in economics, politics, science, and the arts, of being able to shape and master the world, Calvinism was such a powerful cultural influence. We can also understand that a great deal of America's sense of identity and its instinctive feeling that the external world is something "out there" to be tamed and mastered, is derived from this fundamental Calvinist source.

[17] New York: Simon & Schuster, 1956.

really locked in an unwitting embrace in their common repudiation of the Calvinist spirit. Neither is anxious to reshape the world. Both accept it as it is, the conformist manipulating himself within it, the beat saying bad things about it and leaving it for his own kind of monasticism.[18]

The Christian ethic, in modern Protestantism at least, has usually assumed the truth of the Calvinist position. Here is the Christian faith; out there is the world. How can we take the one and relate it to the other in such a way that the world is significantly altered? Now every parent, teacher, minister, and student-worker knows that the power of this activist image is rapidly waning with the younger generation. There are a number of possible responses we can make to this death of activism. We can weep and long for the good old days of clear issues and decisive stands. Or we can scold, and urge clever programs to restore the lost zest to turn the world upside down. Or we can face the death of Calvinist activism as a fact of our times, and then try to proceed, without either tears or scolding, to some new forms of acting that may be possible.

This new form of acting may be found in what I am calling a Christian style of life. It does not mean a re-

---

18 Thus when Philip Rieff speaks of a new kind of man emerging in our time, the Freudian man, his words equally apply to the conformist and to the beat: "the trained egoist, the private man, who turns away from the arenas of public failure to reexamine himself and his own emotions." Such a man is "anti-heroic, shrewd, carefully counting his satisfactions and dissatisfactions, studying unprofitable commitments as the sins most to be avoided." *Freud: The Mind of a Moralist* (New York: Viking Press, 1959), pp. 4, 356.

fusal to act, but it is an attempt to see if the Lutheran tradition cannot be restated and made into a compelling style of life that has its own appropriate action. If the difference between Calvin and Luther can be oversimplified into a difference between an active and a passive style of participating in the world, is it possible to turn to Luther and to a passive style of life without tumbling into the countless dangers that beset us? Can the secular saint for our time be identified by his receiving, his waiting, his suffering? What does this mean?

THE STYLE OF LIFE—A FULLER PORTRAIT

Let us begin by looking at the tension between rebellion and resignation. This is one of the dominant tensions in modern culture's understanding of itself. And most of our pundits, Christian and non-Christian, are for the first and against the second. The classic biblical expression of this tension is found, of course, in the words of Jesus at Gethsemane: "he fell on the ground and prayed that, if it were possible, the hour might pass from him. And he said 'Abba, Father, all things are possible to thee; remove this cup from me; yet not what I will, but what thou wilt'" (Mark 14:35-6). The Gethsemane story is many things, but today it has come to have an uncanny power over us precisely because it is the place in Jesus' life where the rebellion-resignation tension is found in an acute form. Jesus submits himself to God's purpose only after a word of rebellion against it has been openly expressed. Our style of life will always need both of these movements, but rebellion is defended too much and too imprecisely, and resignation, because it looks so much like dread conformity, is scarcely defended at all.

Americans are supposed to be born rebels. Our country began in an act of courageous rebellion, and until recently we seemed to look at the world as something that can be readily changed, if only the right "plan" or method can be found. It is supposed to be an American instinct to rebel when the economic or political orders become unjust. And in our attitude to the world of nature, if there is something we do not know, we have traditionally rebelled against our ignorance. Rebellion against an unsatisfactory world is a common trait of both the traditional American and the Marxist.

But today, as everybody is observing, the classical American image of the rebel, the frontiersman pushing back the barrier that separates the known from the unknown, is becoming fuzzy and confused. The TV Western no longer makes clear distinctions between the good guy and the bad guy, and it is harder and harder to locate just what it is we are supposed to be rebelling against. Politics as rebellion has disappeared, except on the extreme right, to be replaced by a politics of manipulation and adjustment to the possible.

Thus, even though my main purpose in setting forth this rebellion-resignation polarity is to say a good word for resignation, rebellion must be saved from its careless and imprecise defenders. There is still one area of our lives where the Calvinist-activist mood of rebellion can be put to work, at least by the younger generation. This

is the rebellion of the young against the old, against the
family, against the father. What does this kind of rebellion mean?

Hamlet, it may be claimed, is a tragedy of a young
man who did not dare to rebel against the father. He
obeyed his father's command to blood revenge, and this
obedience destroyed him. Cordelia, on the other hand,
made a true act of rebellion in response to her father's
capricious demand for love. She was destroyed, but she
achieved reconciliation at the end. *King Lear*, we might
say, is really a study in how the present must always
break with the past in order to become conscious of itself.
We must repudiate "the father": the past, authority, because it has sinned against us. But like Cordelia at the
end of the play, we must learn, after the rebellion, to
forgive and to love, for this past is what has given us our
lives. *King Lear*, like the Gethsemane story itself, insists
on the presence of both rebellion and resignation, and
thus gives us a clue to the tragedy of *Hamlet*, which is
a tragedy of resignation and conformity to the father.[19]

Rebellion there still can be. We must rebel against the
father, and against everything for which the father is a
symbol: the past, tradition, authority as coercive, even
religion and the church. As we have already seen, some
of us may even need to rebel against God, to accuse him
of injustice or impotence or irrelevance, in order to
come to know who he is. Rebellion of this kind may be

---

[19] I am using here some remarks by Harold C. Goddard, *op. cit.*,
pp. 524-25.

the only way of being honest with ourselves, and for many in our time it will be the only way religious faith can come, if it can come at all. Rebellion against the father can be a means both of self-knowledge and of knowledge of God.

To live in rebellion is dangerous. Many will be unable to bear the loneliness that it may involve, and many will falsely take such an invitation as merely an excuse for conventional bohemianism or irresponsibility. It is difficult, but it is also necessary for many. For many of us the one thing we know is that we cannot give God our full obedience until we have made this act of rebellion against him.

So, rebellion today must be rescued from its false friends, reinterpreted or defended, and then declared inadequate. It was the first word in the Gethsemane story, but it was not the last. "Yet not what I will, but what thou wilt!" What can this mood of resignation or acceptance possibly mean for a Christian style of life? "If you haven't the strength to impose your own terms/ Upon life, you must accept the terms it offers you." Thus speaks one of the characters in T. S. Eliot's *The Confidential Clerk*. Or the prayer of Reinhold Niebuhr, destined perhaps to be the most famous lines he ever wrote, carried in chaplains' kits throughout World War II, and the motto now for Alcoholics Anonymous: "O Lord, grant me the serenity to accept things I cannot change, the courage to change the things I can, and the wisdom to know the difference." Albert Schweitzer defends the wisdom of passivity in even stronger terms.

True resignation consists in this: that man, feeling his
subordination to the course of world-happenings, wins
his way to inward freedom from the fortunes which
shape the outward side of his existence. Inward freedom means that he finds strength to deal with everything that is hard in his lot, in such a way that it all
helps to make him a deeper and more inward person,
to purify him, and to keep him calm and peaceful.
Resignation, therefore, is the spiritual and ethical affirmation of one's own existence. Only he who has
gone through the stage of resignation is capable of
world-affirmation.[20]

At first glance, this mood seems quite foreign and
strange to one brought up in an American or a Christian
tradition of activism. It sounds mystical, oriental, non-
political, escapist, and perhaps even reactionary. Yet as
we reflect, we can see that resignation is just as genuinely a means to knowledge as rebellion is. Rebellion requires freedom and, if it is successful, wins more freedom
for others. But this is only a freedom to do and to act,
a freedom from what fetters and impairs freedom. As
Schweitzer notes, however, there is another kind of freedom just as desirable: freedom within a world, some
parts of which rebellion cannot alter. This kind of freedom is won, not by action, but by a very careful kind of
acceptance and resignation.[21] This kind of freedom, fur-

---

[20] From *Out of My Life and Thought*, by Albert Schweitzer.
Copyright 1933, 1949, by Holt, Rinehart & Winston, Inc. Reprinted
by permission of the publishers. Pp. 257-58.

[21] "To turn to a different point, not only action, but also suffering
is a way to freedom. The deliverance consists in placing our cause

thermore, is not in opposition to discipline; it requires discipline of will and desire. This is the way one comes to live with one's own personal imperfections, and even tragedies; this is the way vocational ambition of a distorted kind is checked; this is the way one is freed for one's work and play by accepting the structures within one's life that are given and unalterable. Now we may make mistakes as to what is and is not alterable. But this distinction can and must be made, as Niebuhr's prayer implies. The strange thing that happens, of course, is that sometimes this acceptance not only accepts but alters the imperfection. The right kind of resignation or passivity often "proves to have been an active attempt at liquidating passivity by becoming fully acquainted with it." [22]

The role of resignation can be seen in the presence of death. Not death in general, but as we face, let us say, a terminal illness in one we love. This disease and this inevitable death must first be taken as an enemy. Doctors fighting the illness must surely rebel against it, and the dying person himself will quite rightly fight, rebel, refuse to give up. But somewhere along the line, the mood of rebellion may shift to a mood of acceptance and resignation. Very often the dying man himself comes to this, and is able to help the bereaved family watching him die. We cannot creatively face the inevitable death of loved

---

unreservedly in the hands of God. Whether our deeds are wrought in faith or not depends on our realization that suffering is the extension of action and the perfection of freedom. That, to my mind, is very important and very comforting." Bonhoeffer, *Letters and Papers from Prison*, p. 173.

[22] Erik Erikson, *Young Man Luther*, p. 157.

ones or ourselves unless we somehow find our way to this mood of resignation and acceptance. We ought not to accept any death too piously or too soon. It is right to cry out, with Dylan Thomas, as he watched his atheist father grow pious on his death-bed:

> Do not go gentle into that good night,
> Old age should burn and rave at close of day;
> Rage, rage, against the dying of the light.[23]

When resignation does come, it will often have been through this kind of rage.

But acceptance or resignation is not only something to call on in the presence of difficulties. It is a way of self-knowledge quite apart from the unchangeable difficulties of life. Erikson, speaking of Luther, writes:

> Paradoxically, many a young man (and son of a stubborn one) becomes a great man in his own sphere only by learning that deep passivity which permits him to let the data of his competency speak to him. As Freud said in a letter to Fliess, "I must wait until it moves in me so that I can perceive it...." This may sound feminine, and, indeed, Luther bluntly spoke of an attitude of womanly conception—*sicut mulier in conceptu*. Yet it is clear that men call such attitudes and modes feminine only because the strain of paternalism has alienated us from them; for these modes are any organism's birthright, and all our partial, as well as our

---

[23] *The Collected Poems of Dylan Thomas* (New York: New Directions, 1957), p. 128.

total, functioning is based on a metabolism of passivity and activity.[24]

Erikson's identification of the passive or accepting style of life with the feminine is very important, and I shall shortly return to this. Here we need merely to say that a style of life for our time will see both the difficulties and the possibilities of rebellion, but will not read the Christian life merely as one of rebellion. It will try to walk warily through the unfamiliar dangers of resignation, and build them into the fabric of the way one stands and acts in a difficult world.

As we have already observed, the distinction between the conformist and the beat styles of life is by no means the same as this distinction between resignation and rebellion. The conformist may be said to have resigned himself to this culture and its ways, but there is often some genuine, if concealed, creativity in his resignation. On the other hand, if true rebellion requires real knowledge of the world it rejects and some kind of concern to transform it through rebellion, the beat very largely fails as a rebel. Lawrence Ferlinghetti's poem "Christ Came Down," [25] to take an example, is apparently intended as a slashing attack on the commercialization of Christmas, but it turns out to be as banal as any ecclesiastical pronouncement or pious holiday editorial on the same subject.

But there is a real issue embedded in the opposition be-

---

[24] *Young Man Luther*, pp. 207-8.
[25] Cf. reference on p. 87 above.

tween the conformist and the beat, even if it is not the resignation-rebellion polarity. It is the problem of just what a break with culture ought to look like. There are two ways of making such a break, the open and the concealed. The open break has great temptations: it is dramatic, visible, and easily praised. It often involves a search for the one, single, solitary act that will dramatically symbolize the rejection. Schweitzer's decision at the beginning of this century to go to Africa is an example of an open break with culture, and the longing of many in our time for such a decisive act is demonstrated by the steady stream of journalists, pilgrims, sophisticated Western men and women of all kinds, to his hospital center. Somehow, we reason, if we can see him, part of the power of his rejection may rub off on us.

The concealed break with culture is more difficult in many ways. It may permit us too easily to go on as before, deceiving ourselves into thinking that we can live in the culture and think bad thoughts about it as our particular form of secret rebellion. Even though a concealed break does not have the dramatic power and visibility of the open one, it must have some visible form to be authentic.

This distinction between the open and the concealed break with culture is an important one. It helps us to identify the true difference between the conformist and the beat, and it is the real way to set forth the polarity between rebellion and resignation as competing styles of life. Even at the risk of seeming to offer a bourgeois or conformist apologia, I would like to defend the con-

cealed break as a mark of the life-style here being described. The open-break tradition is dependent on what
can be roughly described as the existentialist reading of
the human situation, which tells us that modern man's
key experiences are those of being lost, alone, trapped,
unable to escape. Such a reading of our inner experience
requires, therefore, a search for the odd, the extreme, the
unique experience of meaning, as the only way to escape
from the trap, the dark room, the bondage. The answer
is always, in one way or another, a leap. This may mean
a trip: to the Spanish civil war, to Paris, to a Zen monas-
tery. Just as the leap required in Kierkegaard the rejection of his love for Regina, so today this search for the
open break implies a rejection of what is familiar, intimate, small, close at hand.

Now if the contemporary existentialist version of our
experience is imperfect and incomplete, as I think it is,
then there may be something illusory about the direction
the escape has taken. Bonhoeffer has written:

> I have come to be doubtful even about talk of "bor-
> ders of human existence." Is even death today, since
> men are scarcely afraid of it any more, and sin, which
> they scarcely understand any more, still a genuine
> borderline? It always seems to me that in thus talking
> we are only seeking anxiously to make room for God.
> I should like to speak of God not on the borders of
> life but at its centre, not in weakness but in strength,
> not, therefore, in man's death and suffering but in his
> life and prospering. On the borders, it seems to me

> better to hold our peace and leave the insoluble un-
> solved.[26]

This suggests that there may be something theologically
wrong with the style of life that looks only for the extreme or the unique act to give life meaning. Perhaps one
of the ways that passivity or resignation can be built into
our styles of life is to turn from the search for the odd
to a recovery of the familiar. If the secular saint is the
man who lives fully in the world as a man among men,
then will he not have to come to accept the routine, the
lonely city, the intimate—to take his bearings from the
things he touches and sees, day in and day out, and to
build his life on these?

To escape from the broken world? Or to return to it,
and, returning, to make an inner break with it while
suffering calmly its sorrows and joys? I am suggesting
that there is something to be said for the latter. This issue
is vividly portrayed in the second act of Eliot's *The
Cocktail Party*, as we watch first Edward and Lavinia,
and later Celia, receive a healing word from the psychi-
atrist-priest, Harcourt-Reilly. Edward and Lavinia have
watched their marriage disintegrate, each has broken off
an affair with another partner, and each finds he can
live neither with nor without the other. Deeply aware
of their disturbance, they confess before Reilly that they
have no way to go. Reilly helps Edward see that he is
incapable of loving anyone, and helps Lavinia admit that

---

[26] *Letters and Papers from Prison*, p. 124.

no one is capable of loving her. On this basis, much to their surprise, the two decide to return to their conventional life, making the best of a bad job, as Edward puts it. "Your business," Reilly tells Edward, "is not to clear your conscience, but to learn how to bear the burdens on your conscience." The two return, and not until we see them in the final act, giving cocktail parties as before, but acting with a new gentleness toward one another, with Lavinia probably pregnant, do we understand that theirs has been a true way of salvation.

Then Celia, Edward's former mistress, comes to the psychiatrist. Reilly suggests the possibility of her return to the ordinary life of London, describing for her the life to which Edward and Lavinia have returned:

> Reilly: If that is what you wish,
>   I can reconcile you to the human condition,
>   The condition to which some who have gone
>   as far as you
>   Have succeeded in returning. They may re-
>   member
>   The vision they have had, but they cease to
>   regret it,
>   Maintain themselves by the common routine,
>   Learn to avoid excessive expectation,
>   Become tolerant of themselves and others,
>   Giving and taking, in the usual actions
>   What there is to give and take. They do not
>   repine;
>   Are contented with the morning that separates
>   And with the evening that brings together
>   For casual talk before the fire

>   Two people who know they do not under-
>   stand each other,
>   Breeding children whom they do not under-
>   stand
>   And who will never understand them.

Celia: Is that the best life?

Reilly: It is a good life. Though you will not know
            how good
        Till you come to the end.... In a world of
            lunacy,
        Violence, stupidity, greed . . . it is a good life.[27]

Celia, who has been deeply damaged by the conventional world that Reilly here describes, and who, in her
affair with Edward, had received a vision of how genuine
mutuality is really possible between two people, is unable to accept this life. Reilly describes an unknown second way, one that "requires faith—the kind of faith that
issues from despair." Celia asks "Which way is better?"
and Reilly replies, "Neither way is better. Both ways are
necessary. It is also necessary to make a choice between
them." Celia chooses the second, and at the close of the
play we hear that her decision had taken her as a mis-
sionary nurse to Africa, where she was crucified.

Celia, the existentialist heroine, required the odd,
unique, decisive gesture, and she is easy to love and to
identify with. She is the "modern man" of all our theo-

---

[27] *The Cocktail Party.* Copyright 1950, by T. S. Eliot. Reprinted by
permission of Harcourt, Brace & World, Inc.

logical books. Edward and Lavinia did not need what Celia needed; they returned to the world. There will always be need for the radical and dramatic break with a broken world, but it is not the only Christian way, and it is not necessarily the more desirable or the more difficult way. We need to learn to appreciate that Edward and Lavinia have chosen a true way of salvation, the more difficult perhaps, just because it is neither dramatic, obvious, nor noticeable. It is passive rather than active; it is nearer resignation than rebellion. But such a decision can involve genuine heroism, and may be part of a style of life that we badly need to learn.

I have been deliberately imprecise in working out the ways in which the particular style of life defended here can be called Christian. In our time, we have learned a great deal about how to live from secular culture and the secular sources for this style of life ought not to be concealed. One adopts a style of life, if such language is not too voluntaristic, for many reasons that are hidden from us, and only partly, I am sure, because the style can be inferred from this or that Christian insight. I suspect that this style will seem good to some, and, seeming good, it will suggest ways in which the Christian faith can illuminate it. The Christian sources of it are there; they may be partly concealed, and each of us will find his own way of describing them.

The choices of a life-style open to a Christian today, therefore, can be located along a kind of ethical spectrum. At one end are rebellion, activism, transforming the world, the experience of being trapped, and the search for the open and visible break with conformist culture. At the other end are resignation, passivity, receiving and suffering in the world, the search for a concealed break within culture. Many intangibles play into our decision here, and no one of us is so wholly free in this choice as he would like to believe. My main task has been to make a case for the values contained along the passive end of the spectrum, partly because these seem to me genuinely Christian values, partly because most of the interesting art, ethics, and literature of our time is busily engaged in describing or defending, with great plausibility, the values at the other end.

Marriage as a Clue

The simplest way I know to describe these two sets of values is to see them as reflected in the polarity between the male and the female. Is it possible today to make any sense by calling for a rediscovery of the "female" dimension to our ethical experience, and to suggest that a real solution to this entire problem of the active and the passive lies in marriage?

Culturally, there are reasons for being skeptical about this approach. We seem to be living in a time of the death of love, in which there is a terrible breakdown of genuine communication between the sexes. How can we use the man-woman relation, which everyone desires and few really know, to sum up our ethical argument? Leslie Fiedler has recently written a long book claiming that the classic tradition in American fiction has persistently shied away from portraying a full man-woman relation. Huck Finn flees from the womenfolk; the Cooper hero moves away from the women into the forest; the Hemingway male may play with the woman, as with a toy, but the reality of life is found in the battlefield or the bull ring.[28]

These are the cultural reasons that may be given for the foolishness of our hope that the man-woman relation can illuminate our ethical situation. There are also theological reasons why the man-woman relation is suspect. Even though Dr. Barth is able at one point to identify the *imago Dei* in man with his sexuality, his capacity for a relation to the opposite sex, he can still utter this kind of warning:

> The event of sex cannot be considered at all as the sign of divine *agape* which seeks not its own and never fails. It is the work of willing, achieving, creative, sovereign man, and as such points elsewhere than to the majesty of the divine pity. Therefore the virginity of Mary, and not the wedlock of Joseph and Mary, is the sign of revelation and of the knowledge of the mystery of Christmas.[29]

---

[28] Leslie Fiedler, *op. cit.*, esp. p. xix.

[29] *Church Dogmatics* (Edinburgh: T. & T. Clark, 1956), Vol. I, Part 2, p. 192. It is interesting to set alongside this statement another, from Reinhold Niebuhr: "The sexual union as a parable, symbol, and basis for *Agape* has been little appreciated in Christian thought partly because of a generally negative attitude toward sex which Christianity absorbed from the Greek thought; and partly because the particularity of the sexual union is suspect from the standpoint of Christian universalism." *Christian Realism and Political Problems* (New York: Charles Scribner's Sons, 1953), p. 169.

Barth is rightly concerned to protect the free and sovereign character of divine grace and love, and probably fears that the use of sex as a symbol for that love would suggest the possibility of co-operation, and even union, between man and God.[30] But I don't think we need to be dissuaded from our task by these words. Barth is arguing against an analogical use of sexuality to illuminate God's love for man, and in some ways he may be correct. And he is partly right in describing the female as passive, the male as active, in sexuality.[31] But it is the man-world re-

-----

[30] And yet, what would Barth as theologian say to Barth as Mozartian when he listens to the concluding words of the first-act duet "Bei Maennern," from *The Magic Flute*?

Mann und Weib und Weib und Mann
Reichen an die Gottheit an.

"Man and wife and wife and man, follow their Creator's plan"—in the Auden-Kallman translation; or, "Wife and man and man and wife, reach the heights of godly life." But the German is tricky. *Anreichen* apparently means that one thing touches another thing, so that on one end it is really there, while at the other end it is somewhere else. Some kind of God-marriage analogy is really proposed in those words; in marriage there is real participation in God, as well as something less exalted. There is in marriage a giving and receiving, a real knowing and a not-knowing of the other, a sense of being given more than one deserves or expects. This particular duet is partly comic, and the relation between Papageno and Pamina is quite non-sensual and spiritual. But the music is so persuasive that it can almost convince even the most stubborn rejecter of all analogies for God that perhaps this one may be allowed.

[31] "The processes of impregnation, pregnancy, childbirth, and lactation have a certain passivity about them; they are things which *happen* to a woman more than things that she *does*. The sexual act itself, for example, has for her this basically passive quality. The woman, of course, *may* take an active role, but it is not necessary for her to do so, either to satisfy the man or to fulfil her reproductive function." Valerie S. Goldstein, "The Human Situation: A Feminine

lation, not the man-God relation, I am seeking to illuminate with the male-female polarity. So in spite of the dangers, it may be useful to plunge ahead into whatever foolishness may prove to be useful.

I suspect we have not said enough about the sexual act when we make the conventional distinction between the active male and the passive female. There is also a mutuality, a giving and receiving back and forth of these elements. The active one receives by becoming passive, the passive one actively gives in her passivity. Human sexuality finds that the willing, achieving, sovereign male must finally surrender, wait, give himself to the other. This is, I think, a deeper truth than Barth has suggested. And if it is so, the man-woman relation—if it cannot become a symbol for God's love for us—can at least become a symbol for our relation to the world.

It may be, therefore, that neither cultural nor theological difficulties should persuade us to discard the man-woman relationship as a pointer to a special quality in the Christian style of life we are trying to defend and describe. But it is to marriage rather than to sex itself that we must point for our particular clue. Marriage is ordinarily, in the Christian tradition, treated as one of the orders of creation that ought to receive the Christian ethic. It is, I think, more. It is in a very real sense a clue to the meaning of that ethic, or at least to the re-

View," *The Journal of Religion,* XL, No. 2 (April, 1960), p. 104. This is a very interesting article, partly a criticism of the too "masculine" analyses of man and his sin in modern theology, and partly a description of the increasingly feminine quality of our culture.

lationship between rebellion and resignation, the active
and the passive, the Calvinist and the Lutheran postures
before the world. If we were to take sexuality alone as
our clue, we might be tempted to separate too sharply
the active male and the passive female. In marriage, we
have the place in our culture where the male not only
gives but receives, and the female gives as well as receives. In sexuality apart from marriage, there is no necessity for the male to participate in the feminine side of
life. Marriage is what permits sexuality to become a clue
to a wider area of personal and ethical relationships. What
Leslie Fiedler has said of marriage could in no way be
said of sexuality alone. Marriage stands, he writes,

> traditionally not only for a reconciliation with the di-
> vided self, a truce between head and heart, but also for
> a compromise with society, an acceptance of responsi-
> bility and drudgery and dullness.[32]

Marriage is that structure in which a man comes to terms
with the feminine, with the receiving, accepting, suffering side of existence. In marriage a man learns decisively
what it is to be a man; he also learns what being a woman
means, and in some sense he learns actually to be a
woman. We are told today that the image of the father
is becoming blurred in our culture, as he takes over tasks
around the home traditionally associated with the woman.
This is called a bad thing by sociologists, but it is perhaps

---

[32] *Op. cit.*, pp. 330-31. This is the reason, Fiedler notes, why the
American writer fears it, for he fears the maturity or the resignation
that it requires of him.

a good thing ethically, for it may show that he not only understands the feminine but actually participates in it. In sex and marriage, of course, he is finally given the meaning of his true maleness, but he is also given an insight into the essentially female quality in all of life.

If we require a fresh interpretation of passivity, an acceptance of the dullness and routine of life, a rediscovery of the mundane and the familiar as the soil out of which a genuine life-style emerges, then we are in a position to say that marriage may be the one place in our culture that has the power to teach the troubled, Calvinist, activist male the meaning of this. Here he can learn resignation and passivity by learning what it is to be a woman, by refusing to require that his wife become just a different kind of man. Here he may come to see that just as his marriage requires for its success that the woman be related to him in her difference from him, in a like manner his own life requires—as marriage itself requires—the passive along with the active style. The New Testament works out, with some care, the man-woman relation as illuminating the relation between Christ and the church. Here we are adding to this the suggestion that the man-woman relation may also help us understand something about man's relation to the world.

In one sense this style of life may be seen as a very tentative kind of imitation of Christ. We have seen how important were the themes of suffering and humiliation in Christ's life and death. In another sense, it is possible to speak of an imitation of Mary. Mary is reported to have been rebellious, or at least skeptical, at the angel's first approach to her (Luke 1:29, 34), though finally she humbly receives his word (1:38). Perhaps the truly Protestant understanding of Mary might see her as suggesting, both in rebellion and resignation, the relation of the Christian to the world. She is mediatorial, therefore, only in the sense that the secular saint is mediatorial in the world, only as he is a Christ to his neighbor.

I am convinced that one of the most inexhaustible, significant, and hopeful sentences written in our time is that of Bonhoeffer already referred to: "Man is challenged to participate in the sufferings of God at the hands of a godless world." The man who loves God and loves the world enough to do this, will not only have to know how to fight the godless world; he will also need to learn the discipline of resignation and of waiting. To a man, the meaning of this discipline may only come as he comes to know, with difficulty, what a woman knows more naturally. This is why I have suggested that marriage is not only one of the structures of society that needs to receive a Christian word. It is also an important clue to what part of that Christian word ought to be.

* * *

This book has ranged widely, and rather diffusely, over many areas of Christian thought, trying to suggest that there is a way of using a small and very limited set of theological tools with which to do our thinking and our living today. We have chosen a certain way of standing in the midst of our culture, and for this reason some valuable parts of the Christian tradition have been hidden, and even ignored. But perhaps some other parts of that tradition have become more precious or more visible than before. The "essence" we have ended up with is something less than a fully confident Christian perspective from which to launch an all-out attack on a godless world. But it involves enough for us to get on with, and it can give us a style of life permitting us not only to understand and suffer with this world, but actually to enjoy it. I know that this style of life is not the only possible one available today, and I know that its form is both limited and determined in all kinds of ways. But I think the way it suggests we relate ourselves to the world is a true way, and I think it makes as much sense as any other style of life now being offered to us. This essence of Christianity, and the style of life related to it, will doubtless not do at all for tomorrow. But it may do today, and it is in this day we are asked to think, to live, and to obey God.